A DOG'S OWN STORY

By

Thomas Healy

About the Author

I met Thomas about 20 years ago at the Edinburgh Book Festival. He was a tall man in his fifties, quietly spoken, and there was a mutual attraction between us. At this meeting, I could never have guessed what an unusual, adventurous life he had led. He was a bachelor and never wanted to be tied or make commitments, but he loved casual romances. He himself said that he had always been too fond of the lassies. He told me that he was born in the Gorbals and lived with his mother, father, and his sister Mary. He was surrounded by Irish relatives and remembers his granny as an old witchlike woman, dressed in black, smoking her clay pipe, with her kitchen always full of visiting Irish cronies.

Thomas had a happy childhood playing in the streets and going for his weekly visit on a Saturday morning to the Ritz Cinema with Mary and his friend William. He said himself that he was the dunce of his class but was very popular and excelled in all sports and became captain of the school football team. A turning point in his life came when coming back from playing football, elated, as he had just been selected to go for a trial for the Scottish youth team; he was met with the news that his father had died of a massive heart attack aged 46 years.

Thomas never played football again and never went to the trials. His mother and sister were distraught, and his home became a house of mourning. He had become very close to his father in the last year as he had changed bedrooms and now shared with his father and Mary with her mother.

At night his father would regale him with stories of his time in the army, how he had been their champion boxer, and his holidays to Galway as a boy. In the last years of his life, he became very religious. He insisted that the family say the Rosary every evening, with Mary and Thomas secretly making funny faces at each other.

Now, after his death, Thomas roamed the streets at night with no discipline, and he was lucky he avoided the gangs and spent his time frequenting boxing gyms. After his father's death, his mother got a job as a dinner lady. From then on, the food was plentiful as she could bring the leftovers home. Sometimes, when the electricity bill was unpaid, his mother sent them to the chapel, and the priest gave them some candles, which they loved when sitting at night in their candlelit kitchen, but his mother was ashamed that the neighbours would notice. Thomas always said that his father's death changed his life's direction.

Preface

I heard Thomas talking to mammy telling her that we were going to Cornwall for a break. It was a long coach journey but we stopped at Birmingham for a rest and Thomas was well prepared with food and drink for both of us. When we arrived in Bude, the coach stopped next to the local pub "The long John Silver", where we were to collect the caravan key. The proprietor said it was about ten minutes' walk away along a narrow lane, which he pointed out and across a field. By this time, it was dark but there was a big full moon which lighted our way. I did not care where I was as long as I was with my big pal Thomas, I would have followed him to the ends of the earth. We soon saw the site with a few scattered caravans, and Thomas said that we'd be better going straight to bed and getting a good night's sleep after our long journey. I yawned and nodded in agreement. We slept together, me at the foot of the bed and him at the top. When I awoke, I could hear Thomas outside talking to some floozy. It didn't take **him** long! He invited her in and I pretended I was asleep, and she cooed, "Oh what a big darling," and tried to pat me. I growled my most fierce growl and she screamed and jumped back, "Oh," she said, "I'm a bit scared of big dogs." Thomas reassured her and said that I was usually a big pussy cat! The cheek of him. I gave another big fierce growl and she backed quickly away and hurriedly said that she'd better leave and they could meet up that night at The Long John Silver.

***

We went for a long walk, I was in the huff and pretended not to enjoy it. When we got back, he quickly slapped down my meal on the floor, but I turned my head away and refused to eat it. "Martin, have it your own way, there's no need to sulk, a man has his needs, it's my holiday too. He spent ages sprucing himself up and finally said, "Martin, will I do?" I turned away and shut my eyes; I felt betrayed. Imagine him leaving me alone on our first night in a strange caravan. Luckily his floozy was leaving the next day as this was the end of her holiday. Good riddance! The two of us were together again, pals. Every day we explored the area and walked in a different direction each day. We usually covered about ten miles at least and I was allowed to run free. Sometimes when there were sheep about Thomas would put my lead on. Silly Thomas. I had no intention of chasing those stupid woolly creatures. Though now and again, for fun, I would give a loud bark and they would scatter. "Now Martin, there's no need for that." Thomas carried a big bag on his back containing a bowl of water and Chappie for me and sandwiches and a flask of coffee for him. Then he would relax against a tree and roll himself a smoke. He kept of the strong booze for quite a few days. I think he was trying to make up to me for the floozy. Thank goodness it let me relax more. returning to the caravan. He had no sense of direction and relied on me to find our way back, though by then it was very dark but I could sniff my way back easily. Starlit nights! But if he had been on his own, he'd have been hopelessly lost, even when sober. Just as well I was not a drunk. At night we would amble down to the pub which I didn't mind if he stuck to a few beers. One night he said, "Martin, I think I'll try the local brew, Scrumpy, a rough sort of cider, it's cheap and the locals seem to like it." The other drinkers must have thought he was mad talking to a dog, but of course they didn't know that I was a special dog. He downed a few bottles, one was never enough once he got the taste of it and eventually, we left; him carrying a bag of clinking bottles. I felt like tripping him up to break them, but while the money lasted, he'd just buy more. He had laughed when he read the label, "Happy, but legless." He was half drunk already. A strong brew. And **he** soon would be legless.

***

After managing to stagger back he fed me and said, "Martin, it's a lovely night I'll take you for another walk." My heart sank, whose kidding, it would be me taking **him** for a walk. After about five minutes he staggered down a grassy slope beside a brook. He settled himself down on the grass and I lay down beside him. After a few bottles, he fell into a drunken sleep and there was nothing for it but to keep guard all night. When the sun came up, I began to lick his face to wake him up. He awoke with a groan, holding his head, and had no clue where he was. He began to scrabble around the long rough grass and found a few empty bottles. "Thank God," he said when he found an unopened bottle," Someone must be looking over me," he quickly gulped it down in a oner and I growled in disapproval. "At least it didn't rain, Martin, but nobody but you and I will know of this."

***

Thomas, for the next few days was back on the fire water, not eating and forgetting to feed me regularly and leaving me to forage for myself He finally sobered up and said, "Martin, we're in a bit of a fix, I've the return coach tickets to get home to mammy, but no money to pay for the caravan I should have paid for it at the start. There's no way we can leg it as the coach pick-up point is right outside the pub." I tried to look sympathetic, but it was him who had spent all the money on strong drink. "There's nothing for it, we'll need to rob the wishing well. It will be a great adventure." I nodded my head wisely, "Let's hope we don't get caught" but so did I, what would happen to me if my big pal was sent to jail? We had seen the wishing well in Bude on our walks and it was full of coins. We stole out in the early hours of the morning, he had cut down on the booze the whole day and was nearly sober. He had acquired a jemmy from outside a plumber's yard. The wishing well was a round stone structure, and the custom was to throw coins for luck, good luck for us. There was a metal grid with a small padlock attached and at the bottom of the well was about a foot of water and a treasure of glinting coins." You stay on guard", It was a bright, moonlit night and Thomas wished it was cloudy for better cover. He jerked with the jemmy and finally after a struggle the padlock snapped off and clanged onto the grating. It sounded like thunder in the still night. "Keep a lookout, Martin, someone could have heard that." I watched him intently; he had sweat on his brow from his efforts; it was a harder job than he had thought. But soon he was over the wall trying to wrench up the grating, he had to have been at it about fifteen minutes trying to get a grip of it and yank it clear. Finally, it came off. He took off his shoes and socks, rolled up his trouser legs, a paddle in the money. He began to scoop up handfuls of money and stuff them into his pockets. I pricked up my ears as I heard footsteps in the distance. I began to low growl to warn him and he quickly stepped out of the well and snapped on my lead. Suddenly a policeman appeared, on foot, wheeling an old bike, a skinny looking individual. Thomas still had bare feet and trousers rolled up Banged to rights. "What do you think you're up to? I thought the policeman must be really stupid if he couldn't work that out. I began straining at my leash and growling fiercely and was ready to grab the cop by the leg and give him a good bite. He backed away a little and said, "That dog's a threat, keep the fucking thing away from me." I was growling and baring my teeth and when I was like that, I'm quite proud to say I can look real scary. Thomas said quietly, "This dog means the world to me and if I go to jail, what would become of him, so that is not going to happen. Give me a break!" "Is that a threat?" The cop said in a tough voice. He seemed very nervous, no wonder. "Are you Scottish?" Thomas said that he was and only wanted him and his dog to get back safely to Glasgow. "You should be in cuffs." the cop said. Thomas said, "Give me a break". You don't meet many too brave guys in this world, "I've pockets full of coins and plenty more down there and it would get us both out of a sticky situation intact." The cop was in a quandary, he didn't know what Thomas would do but he was well aware what I would do to save my master. Was arresting Thomas worth losing a finger or even a hand? He suddenly made up his mind and told Thomas to put some coins on the ground and walk away and we'll call it quits. Thomas did what he said and without another word, he grabbed his shoes and we turned and walked away without a backward glance. That was the closest I got to losing my big pal, a near thing.

The next morning, Thomas paid the proprietor with a handful of pound coins and he looked very suspicious but must have thought it would be safer not to comment. Probably glad to see the back of us. On the coach Thomas said, "You know I said a prayer we would get home safe and sound and I think that's what saved us"

**

A DOG'S OWN STORY

There were five of us, two girls and three boys, including me. We got along okay. A lot of rough and tumbling, especially after our mother left. It was a sudden departure and I thought she had abandoned us, if I know better now. That she had no choice. I would fancy her to have been most upset, but there was nothing she could do. Not a thing. She had served her purpose and we, her brood, were up for sale: *Doberman pups. Good pedigree. Big boned. Black and tan* £150.

We were five weeks old and unaware of this, that, in time, we would be sold off one by one and would never meet again. It is the lot of the dog, and I can't say that we stood up for one another. Anything but, and feeding times were one mad scramble. A survival of the fittest. Should you be slow at all you would be hungry and I learned how to hold my own at this early stage, which did not escape the attention of our master who would cuff my head because he thought I was eating too much. "A greedy pig," was what he called me, but if he had provided food enough for all of us there would have been no fighting. An idiot would have known that, and I think he liked to watch us fight. In event, I was six weeks old when he first hit me. A big, meaty, hairy hand. I viewed him with caution after that, but my hunger was such that as often as not I risked his wrath. Some messy looking, gruel-like food which, all in one batch, was supplied to us. This in an airless room on a filthy mattress. Not that it stopped us having fun, for we knew no better and there was nothing else for it, anyhow. We were of a kind that is dependent on humanity.

1

Thousands of years have made us so, as, gradually, in Stone Age times, we befriended man. But we have a proud streak still, some of us, or as proud as man will let us be, from our wolf ancestry. The wild untamed. I could sometimes feel it surge in me, even then; against the hand, in our confine. One day to another, and there were other hands that would lift me up and put me down. A babble of voices. I recognised my master's voice, and he was a new man then, patting my head and singing my praises. What a good boy I was. I had come to learn his smell, and did not like the odour. A liar and cheat and a bully to boot. I was often afraid that he would kick in my ribs in a fit of temper. It would have been the end of me, and I wanted to survive. Our cruel master. He had already kicked in one of our sister's ribs and she had died as a result, in a pool of her own lung-blood. Such was my education, start in the world. I was made aware that I was a dog and had no rights at all. None of us had, *have.* We are at the whim of our master; whoever she or he might be, from the beginning to the end. Our time on this earth. It is not long. A decade at best of active life. And that if you are lucky. That you can avoid the brutes in human guise. The man who had killed our sister. He was a true king brute, and we all feared him. A mortal dread. Where we were once five, we were down to four. I vied with my remaining sister for who was the smallest in the pack, not that there was much between us. Our measly rations. We were all half-starved, and that's a fact. I think our master must have stolen us, for he had no idea how to raise a litter and the wonder was that we did not perish. In that stifling room on the filthy mattress. We were still too young to climb from it, to make a run; and where to go even if we could. Our brutal master. He was a silly one too. It is much easier to sell a plump healthy puppy than a skinny bag of bones. What we were, had become, before I was seven weeks old. But resilient too and, one day to the next, I could only hope that I was taken away from this dreadful place. One of my brothers had already been taken, in exchange for – it is the wherewithal amongst the humans - some bits of coloured paper. Our master had been in a fine fettle afterwards, as gloating over the bits of paper and he had fed us a little extra –or it might have been that there was one less mouth to feed and he had forgotten that and provided feed for four instead of three. Whatever, for a change, we had all full bellies and the very next day my luck was in when a strange long-fingered hand picked me up. I liked the smell and clung on to the back of it for all my worth. *Take me with you, please.* There were some harsh words between the owner of the long-fingered hand and my master who was suddenly afraid. Indeed, he was and it was good to see, to *sense*, that he was not so high and mighty now, confronted, as he was, by another, bigger human. An argument concerning me, for how many bits of paper I was worth. I had dug in my claws on the stranger's hand and when my master tried to snatch me back, he was roughly pushed aside. A snarl of rage from *my* hand's owner. It was how I thought, and; whatever way it had come about, whoever owned the hand, was the one I wanted to be with.

***

So it began, my life with Thomas; who put me in his coat pocket. I was such a tiny little thing back then that he could have squashed me to death in the palm of his hand. But I knew no fear and I trusted him then and would continue to trust him throughout the years, as that we were meant to be together. A man and his dog. It sometimes happens, but not too often and not so quickly, and I have often wondered if Thomas knew when he chose me that it was for keeps, my time on this earth.

***

We went home in a taxi. I should mention that wherever he went was now home to me. In his pocket in the taxi, I peeked out, all big brown eyes and little else. I would doubt the driver noticed me. Not that I cared, or would ever care too much about other people. It was not in my nature, not even then. I had found Thomas or he had found me and that would be the way of things, what was meant to be. Me and him. I had clung on to his hand with all my might because, I think, I was the more aware of our fate than he was. Something deep in the root of me, that; after I had whiffed his hand, insisted I should be with him. A dog sense! Well, this *is* a dog's own story, is it not? As best as I can tell it. How it was, and I have to begin when I was a pup and everything was new to me. Thomas's house. He stayed with his mother and sister and I had a bit of a job in winning his mother over. "What does he want with a dog?" she asked.

"It's only a helpless wee pup," the sister defended, and I was glad of that, her defense. "We'll need to keep it in the meantime." The old one considered and shook her head. "I wonder where he got it from."

I should mention that during this conversation I had burrowed in on Thomas's chest, some comfort in the beat of his heart. That he was still alive. It was touch and go, so I thought, until I discovered that he was only drunk. It was a big, the major failing in my new master; his weakness for strong water, and I determined to help him all I could to overcome his problem. It was it was in my own interest along with his if I was to stay with him. The old one whom I now called mammy fed me tins of puppy food while Thomas was indisposed. She cleaned up after me as well, and after I had done my business, I would climb up Thomas's leg and nestle in on his chest again. This unhappy state went on and on until he had no money left. Mammy was pleased and so was I, and his sister. Her name was Mary, and she wore a uniform for her job as a traffic warden. I got along fine with her, but it was mammy who fed me and who was in the house all day, and I loved her second best to Thomas. There was nothing wrong with mammy, I tell you; she had put up with her drunken son for years and now, as all of a sudden, I was there. An untrained, un-named puppy. None of them knew if I was a boy or a girl and I was just hanging in, holding on; for when Thomas finally sobered up, he had to have had misgivings. A sore head. His fingers shook so badly that he could not roll a cigarette, and what-for mammy had made it crystal clear that I was his responsibility - was he to do with me? I was big-eyed looking up at him, as pleading that he did not sell me. I was worth a lot of the wherewithal, and as mammy had said to Mary: "He might sell the wee dog for drink."

Please God, no; don't sell me, Thomas. And neither he did. But it was a shaky time none the less, that I might be sold for him to buy more booze. This was the one and only time he would think about it, selling me. The next time he drank we were much too close and, for my part, I was much bigger, and not so readily saleable. A reversal in our roles. That I had become more of his guardian; a watchful eye, looking out for him. A stupid, befuddled Thomas. I began to hate drink as much or even more than mammy. It turned my master into rubber and he would sometimes fall and when he did, I would stand guard over him.

***

Thomas began to try to train me to walk on a lead when I was nine weeks old. Not that it was much of a lead, more a length of clothes line, and I was still without a collar. All his money had gone on alcohol and he had to beg for tobacco from mammy. Two expensive, bad habits that the big man had. Out on our walks we would sometimes meet with other people and he was sometimes called Big Tam, but I would always think of him as Thomas. Our first few walks were very awkward. I was unused to a lead and people and traffic and, sometimes; here and there, some other dogs, and it was all too much and I would occasionally stop and just sit down. When this happened Thomas would lift me up against his chest –where I felt secure – and carry me back home. But little by little I became used to it and began to look forward to our walks. Mammy bought me my first collar. It was a thin, plastic affair which would not last for very long. But I was grateful for it, as, at last, that I belonged and was accepted in the pack. I think that mammy- I was eleven weeks old by then - had felt sorry for me, that I was so small and helpless and, to begin at least, was dependant on her, not Thomas; who, after he had brought me home, had been barely aware of my existence. But we had come through all that and were still together, and I had slept with him when he had been drunk. When he sobered up there were changes and I was moved out of the bed on to a couch that ran alongside the bed, and this was to be our sleeping quarters for many years to come. Me on the couch and him in bed but close enough, should we wish, to reach out and touch each other.

The sober Thomas was a much different man from the drunken one. No wonder mammy and I, and Mary too, hated it when he got drunk. I can't say that he was strict, it was just not in his nature; not with me, but I was treated with a more firm hand, which I liked. I had had no or little discipline until this time, and I wanted to please and he house trained me in less than a week. His wee dog. It was what Mammy called me, and would continue to call me when I was big, "Thomas's wee dog." And I did my best to walk with him, if it took a bit of doing. A lot of encouragement. Thomas would sit on his haunches and stroke my head and whisper words that made no sense but were very reassuring. The trembling puppy that I was. A bit of fur and bone and big, brown, wondering eyes. Thomas was patient, I'll say that for him; and he never rowed or scolded me, and

7

after a while I began to like to go out walking with him.

***

I had to be about twelve weeks old when Thomas discovered I was a boy. Not that he cared, I don't think. Not then. We had become great pals, but I have to say that it was not the sharpest observation. I would have thought it more than obvious, on a glance, what sex I was and that it was nothing to make a big deal of. This, the sex thing, came about when it was decided I should have a name, and I was dubbed with Tulip. A girl's name, if there ever was one; and I wanted to scream at him that I was a boy. There were times, and this was one, when Thomas could be very dumb. Damn stupid, I would say. The good thing was that Tulip was scrubbed, and I was re-named Martin. A boy's name. I would have felt a terrible fool if I'd been stuck with Tulip.

I clocked on to my new name pretty fast, and so it was, Thomas and Martin and Martin and Thomas, and there sometimes was some confusion about who was who when we were out and meeting with other people. There was one boy, a teenager named Alec, who had one of my breed, a Doberman called Sabre, whom we often met with in a particular field which was fenced off from the road.

Alec was into boxing, and so was Thomas, and they would speak about boxing while I played with Sabre. He was about one year old, was Sabre; and he was lean and hard with long, sharp teeth. I used to watch out for his teeth, but; once we began to know each other, I knew he was okay and it was a delight to see them, him and Alec, in the field where we would sometimes stay for hours. I would have been about three and a half months old then, playing in the field with Sabre. I was born in February so it would have been May, the long bright summer nights. We were both, Sabre and me, full of energy and both of our tails were docked, which was legal then – and I think that a Doberman's tail should be docked, for it makes us look much smarter – and, certainly, it did not, the lack of a tail, affect my balance. Or Sabre's. I would fancy Thomas would think I had been born that way, without a tail; for it was the only way he ever knew me. Alec, for his part; young as he was, would have known differently. He was really into dogs, the Doberman breed, where Thomas was a novice. I should mention here that I was not a tall Doberman, if such a thing exists; for it is a made-up breed that originated in Germany by a man named Louis Doberman. He was out to create the perfect guard dog and succeeded in part, that, even today, given our reputation, people are wary of us. For myself, I was a shade too low, short in the legs; and my chest was thicker and my head bigger than what a Doberman's should be. It did not bother me or Thomas, this imperfection, and I was passed off as a Doberman regardless. It might well be that I was three quarters Doberman with a bit of a Spitz flung in. God knows, I don't; and it hardly mattered anyhow, and no-one was about to tell Thomas that I was less than perfect. Sabre used to drop down on his front paws when he saw us coming. A time for play. Hurrah! We'd meet sometimes in the afternoon and again at night, so I had come to know him pretty well, as he did me. Alec and Thomas would speak about a new heavyweight contender named Mike Tyson. As time went on, I would get to know, in a passing way, a German Shepherd dog named Tyson. He was big enough but lacked the grit of his famous namesake. People should begin to understand that every dog has its own nature, and because it is of a certain breed you should not expect too much from it, if it is not *in* it. Sabre was no toughie either. And neither was I when it comes to it, except when guarding Thomas. The difference was that I could hold my own with the best of them, which was more than could be said of Tyson and Sabre. A bad-tempered poodle would have put the fear of death in them.

Despite this; an innate timidity, Alec was more than fond of Sabre and I have to say that I liked him too. He was full of fun and my first playmate. But it was all to come to a bad end when Sabre; he must have seen something that I did not, ran out from the field and, through a space in the railings, on to the open road. Alec called him back, and for a moment Sabre stopped and wide-eyed looked around him. His wild dash. It had taken him out on to the centre of the road, all swerving traffic. A bamboozled Sabre. He stood stock still and Alec ran towards the fence, to stop the traffic, if he could, and rescue Sabre. But it was all too late, and I heard the thud as a van hit Sabre sideways on; smashing him up, and then a bus from behind ran into the van and a car hit the bus and a whole pile-up. On the road. Alec held Sabre's head but blood gushed from his mouth and I knew that he was done for. Much like my sister, when our old master had kicked her ribs in.

10

Thomas led me away, away from the fence. "Come on, Martin," and I could tell that he was really sad at what had happened on the road, the now dead or dying Sabre.

***

"But it could have been worse, it could have been you; and I don't want to lose you, Martin." Thomas sat on my couch and I sat on his lap, snuggling in. "You're the only pal I've got, you know." It was not the first time he had cuddled me, but an extra affection; and I felt warm and glad that he did not want to lose me, for I did not want to lose him either, and then; as such things go, we very nearly did, lose each other when someone poisoned me.

We had a small front garden and I would sometimes play in it alone, without any supervision. I would hardly think to have needed supervision when the garden was wired off from the street and I could not get out until Thomas opened the gate. I would be alone in the garden for the shortest of times, about ten minutes. In the mornings. We would then go round to the open field where I would then do my business. It had become a sort of ritual until, one morning; when I thought my luck was in, I ate a piece of meat. Looking back, I should have sensed that there was something very wrong, fishy about that piece of meat, how; as out of nowhere, it had suddenly appeared. But I trusted to luck and wolfed it down, before Thomas came out and took it from me. What he would have done. So, I thought I was smart and that he knew nothing and as we made our way to the field as usual, I was feeling fine, just dandy; and I forgot all about my poisoned gift until I collapsed in that same field.

"What ails you, Martin?" Thomas asked, but my eyes were so heavy that I could barely even look at him. Mammy said something about a vet.

"He just fell apart," Thomas said. "I don't understand it, mammy." "Then you'd better get him to a vet, the poor wee thing." The vet wore a white coat and felt my tummy and opened my eyes, for they were closed by now, and pronounced that I had been poisoned.

***

"Martin was poisoned in the garden."

"How do you know that?"

"Because it was the only place it could have happened, because it was the only place where he was alone."

Mammy gasped at that. "Who would do such a rotten thing?" Thomas said that he could think of a few. "Somebody trying to get back at me and taking it out on Martin." Mammy was outraged at this, and Thomas- well, had he caught whoever had poisoned me he would have killed them there and then. This was a fact, and he would have gone to jail so it was better all around that he never did find out. "Will the wee dog recover?" Thomas said he didn't know, and that neither did the vet. "He told me some dogs recover but others don't, and gave me a bottle that I have to give to Martin every three hours."

"A *bottle*?"

"It's got a dummy teat."

"I'll say a prayer for Martin."

"He needs all the prayers that he can get going by the looks of him."

"He'll be okay."

"I wish I was so sure."

"Wait and see."

"There's nothing else I can do, mammy."

I remember little of the next few days, such was my delirium. On the couch. But Thomas was with me all the time, I do know that. Every so often he would open my mouth and press the teat on the back of my tongue so that I had to swallow down the medicine. That and he made a big thing of me. "Good boy, Martin. We'll beat this, don't worry." But *he* was worried, all of this fuss, attention. "Alec has bought a new pup, I hear. He's calling him Duke, and he'll be a new pal for you." But the only pal that I was wanted was sitting there right beside me. Something in my sub-conscious. I was far too groggy to feel much pain, and I fouled the couch but Thomas seemed not to care. "I don't want you to leave me, Martin." Off and on mammy might look in and stroke my head, and Mary too, and it was good to know that I was wanted, that they all were rooting for me. Thomas, especially. I was *his* dog, remember. There would never be, when I recovered, be any doubt as to whose dog I was, not that there had been much before. But a new, unshakable bond now forged between

13

us. I was his and he was mine and we didn't give a damn, neither of us, about what anybody thought.

I could feel the joy in Thomas's heart when I first lapped some water. "We've won, Martin; we've won." And so, we had. Within hours of that first sip of water I was down from the couch and back in the living room and a member of our pack again. Mammy and Mary were overjoyed, I think as much for Thomas as for me. It didn't matter, and you could feel the happiness in the house that I had recovered. More or less, for I was still a little shaky. A lot weaker now than I had been before, before that poisoned meat. Thomas told mammy and Mary that I would not be allowed into the garden on my own again. "They won't get another chance at us, whoever poisoned Martin." No, and neither they did; and in short order, three days or four, I was back to my bouncing self, for I was naturally high spirited, inquisitive, full of fun, and Thomas encouraged this. Not for him a cowed, submissive dog. He liked to see me wild and free and I had a pretty loose rein, until, that is, I broke free of my lead one day to chase an Irish Setter.

This Setter lived at the top of our street and was forever outside its house barking at me ferociously. At first, I had been scared and had was glad when Thomas crossed the road in order to avoid it. The problem was that of late it had taken to cross the road to follow us, barking all the while. I think Thomas was fed up with it, and I know I was. That crazy, fool of a dog. I was almost five months old by then, and I could feel my dander getting up for all that Thomas said, "Forget it, Martin." It would have been good if I could, but one of the days something snapped and so did my lead and I was up and after the Irish Setter, meaning business. Thomas stood with the lead in his hand, calling me back, but I ignored him. It was to be a first falling out, for when I did return, he was very angry. The Irish Setter, his name was Kelly, was all noise and nothing else and he had scampered across the road and leapt over the fence into his garden to escape from me. I was not yet big enough to leap the fence after him, so there was nothing else but to return to the upset Thomas who, I know, was surprised by my show of fury. "Bad Martin," he scolded me, and as he was without a lead, I had to follow him back home. Which I did with my head way down, for I knew that I should have come back to him when he had called my name. As for Kelly, he did not bait me anymore. Rather a wide berth. For both me and Thomas, for we went together, as a team; and I was really sorry that I had vexed him so for the mad chase after Kelly.

***

Alex's new dog, Duke, was much more deliberate, steadfast, than his predecessor, the ill-fated Sabre had been. There was little chance that Duke would dash out of the field onto the open road. He was quite without energy and had no heft at all. Indeed, he looked half starved, but I knew he wasn't and that there was something wrong with him. He was three months old and half the size he should have been for his age. To add to this, he was always shaking and I decided to keep my distance from him. At around this time, the Kelly incident and Duke's arrival, I chanced to see my former master when

I was in a park with Thomas. The brute was with a big black dog, which had its head hung down low and was clearly frightened of him. For myself, that murderous bully – I could smell his whiff before I saw him – my ruff went up and I began to growl, alarming Thomas who was seated on a wooden bench. "What's the matter with you, Martin?"

I continued to growl, alerting the brute's attention. He did not look so all powerful now, and I remembered how he had kicked my sister, smashing her ribs and killing her. Thomas, how did not even know the brute; he had been so drunk when he had bought me, said, "Take it easy, Martin." But I could not. No. I felt the growl low in my belly, and I was primed to attack when his arm went round my neck, restraining me; or halfway so for, such was my fury, that I pulled him from the bench on top of me and, in this melee, myself and Thomas, as fighting one another, the murderer escaped unscathed. Which was more than could be said for Thomas, who took a paw full in the eye. What to do, for I did not mean it. Anything but this. I would have given my life for him. "What the fuck is it with you?" he snarled. "What's it all about?"

Of course, I couldn't say, tell him; who, I'm sure, if I could have done, would have understood. As it was, I could only look at him with big pleading eyes. This was one of the few times that I was looking down on Thomas, for he was still on the ground; holding his eye, while I was standing over him, feeling awful; his poor eye, and it was the one time I thought that he might hit me, but rather than that he shook his head: "I sometimes just don't get you, Martin."

"What happened to your eye?"

"Martin hit me with his paw."

"No, he didn't; Martin would never hit you."

"It was an accident. We were playing around, and his paw hit my eye."

I was sitting as far away as I could get, feeling so lousy that I can't explain. My big mate. His wounded eye. It was all red and inflamed and mammy told him that he'd need to go and see about it. "You can't walk about with your eye like that." All this was because of my former master, while Thomas thought it was the big black dog he had with him that I had meant to go for. Not that it mattered, not now; and I wished never to see that *cur* again and could but pity the big black dog he had with him." But mostly I was in mourning. It is the only way I can describe my feelings, loving Thomas as I did. Should he turn against me I might as well curl up and die, for there would be nothing left in the world for me. But he did not. Far from it. The whole thing had been an accident, and we were still good pals when he returned from the hospital. "How's *my* Martin?"

I leapt up on him and he ruffled my hair and I knew this was how it was meant to be, me with him; all down the years. "I've to wear the patch for a couple of weeks," he told mammy. "But the eye's okay, only bloodshot." "Then you were lucky." Mary agreed. "You'll need to be more careful when you play with Martin, because he's becoming big and strong."

"You can say that again, he's becoming strong. I couldn't believe the strength of him when we were playing in the park today." Thomas was now sitting down and I jumped on to his lap, better that I could lick his face. "I don't think Martin knows his own strength."

"But you do, and he's your dog and your responsibility. She was always on about that, was Mary; that I was his dog and his responsibility. "You're all that Martin's got in the world," she said. Thomas was all I wanted in the world. I had known that ever since I had clutched on to the back of his hand and would not let go. No wonder that I licked his face when he returned from the hospital, wearing a shield-like thing over his damaged eye.

"That's true," Mammy said, "and you've got a real pal in Martin." I doubt she would have thought that had she seen us earlier in the park, on the ground; one rolling over the other, like we were in a real fight. Thomas held me back from him, looking into my eyes. "How did I ever come by you?" "Because you got drunk," Mary said, "that's how you came by him." "Then it must have been fate, because I never ever thought of getting a dog before." This talk about me. I wished that I could join in, but I could only bark or growl or howl. Which I did, when Thomas went out without me. A call of the wild, in the city. If we had been in woods, or in the wild, he would have heard my howl and howled back and so, little by little, we'd have found each other. "It might be the only good thing I've ever done when I was drunk," Thomas said, and hearing this I gave his face an extra lick.

Later that night, in our room on my bed Thomas said that we were going to school. "To the Doberman club, Martin." I had my head in his lap, a mutual trust. It was the way we were and Thomas could have beaten me to death and I would have lacked the heart to even try to defend myself against him. "Whatever good it might do, it can't do us any harm." With that Thomas rose and undressed himself and switched off the light and patted my head, "Goodnight, Martin,"

***

The first change that the Doberman club brought about was I now wore a choke chain. This was a length of steel that, should I jerk or pull, would tighten around my neck. I hated the thing for the first few days, but then accustomed to it. It lent a measure of control to Thomas, that I could not pull at him the way I had, almost taking him off his feet chasing after Kelly. It was, it appeared; at the Doberman club, a standard measure that all the dogs wore choke chains. Which was just as well as some of them were quite aggressive, up for fighting. The choke chains put a stop to this, and in that place, and out of it, for that matter – I am thinking here of the humans– they were very, very necessary. You soon wised up to the click of the chain and to work as a team, which suited me. With Thomas. I showed a certain reserve towards the other dogs and humans, some of whom; the humans, had queried our right to be in the school on the grounds that I might not be a true Doberman at all. Well, I might win no prizes in the show department but, and even the trainer remarked on it, that I would have won top award for loyalty. During this time, we still met with Alec and Duke, who rather than grow appeared to diminish. He was really the smallest little dog to have ever been called a Doberman, or even a miniature Pinscher. He stuck close to Alec, who, I think, and after Sabre, could not understand it, the size; or lack of it of it in the trembling Duke. "He should be much bigger than he is."

Thomas said he might grow, but he was kidding no-one; not me, nor Alec, whom; I understand, had had him to a dog doctor. "There might be something wrong with Duke's kidneys." "Poor Alec." Thomas said when we were alone. "I don't think Duke is well at all. And neither did I. A whiff of his breath. It wouldn't have needed a doctor to tell me that Duke's kidneys were not in the best of order. "He might not be long for this world, Martin." I thought the same, and sure enough Duke was not there, in the field, a short time afterwards.

You would have thought, two Dobermans; that it would have been enough for Alec. But no, for another one came on the scene. His name was Caesar, and he was eighteen months old and I was leery of him. For reason, for he was big and a bit of a biter. Nothing serious, but painful nips that I well could do without. He seemed particularly attracted to my ears, which were floppy; hanging down, and before too long I turned on him and bit his nose. He yelped in pain and backed away, and that was the end of his ear nipping. "Good for you;" Thomas said when we had left the field. "That Caesar's a big bully."

He thought I needed telling that? Did he think I was a fool or what? It was not his ears that stung after we had encountered Caesar. However, after a little I became friendly enough with him, Caesar that is. By now I had a metal studded leather collar, the same as all the other dogs at the Doberman school. Come to that, so had Caesar, and he too was a member of the school, where; one night, he caused a fight by biting another dog's ear. Alec seemed to have no luck with the dogs he acquired, and Caesar was a problem from the start. For instance, after a couple more biting incidents they were shown the door at the Doberman school, as the trainer; who was a strong voiced ex-army man, was not prepared to put up with it, Caesar's bad behaviour. Thomas and me we were model pupils, and we would walk it there and walk it back, and I liked my nights at the Doberman school.

***

Thomas was thirty-nine years old when he came by me, or; given a bit more accuracy, I came by him. I know this now, what I did not know then; the strange big drunken man. One would have thought he was not the full shilling, the way he thrust me inside his pocket. Where, as said, I felt to belong, in the company of this strange wild man. He had sorted out my old master with a cuff on the jaw and an order to phone a taxi. For us. My escape. Some might think I was mad to put my trust in such a man. That he could have been more cruel to me than even my old master. I thought not. There was something about him, a vulnerability; that he could not resist

21

affection. I sensed this on the instant, the smell of his hand; and, for I was tenacious if nothing else, that was why I had clung on to it. This pleased him and he stood up for me right there and then, that I was *his*; and it was why he had cuffed my old master, who had tried to snatch me off his hand, when he had asked for extra money.

My old master held a hand to his jaw and we beat a retreat, right of that fetid room. The filthy mattress. One small confession, I did not give a single thought to the ones I had left behind. You have to seize the moment, which I did; on a hunch, it was nothing more, that we should be together. As it was, turned out – and I have explained about his mammy and sister – I was to discover he *was* the full shilling and more, but terribly lonely. A man alone. The booze had almost done for him and he would get into fights and he had given up on his fellow man if I think he still liked women. There was a certain house he would sometimes frequent while I was still a pup. About four or five months old, I think. There were always loud, drunken, females in the house which was owned by a woman called Nancy. We went there a couple of times, during the day, until I had a fight with Nancy's cat, which was a big, striped, long tailed tom. It had a go for my eyes, and I fought back and Nancy and Thomas had a falling out and we never went back to that place again. As for Nancy, she came round to our house late one night when she was full of wine and, I was at the door with Thomas, I was delighted when he told her to get lost in no uncertain terms. So, he had no friends now except for me and mammy and Mary, who were all pack members. Mammy, too, I am glad to say, was glad to see the back of Nancy.

"The brazen lump," she said. "I hope nobody saw her coming to our door at this time of night."

So that was it, whatever had been with Thomas and Nancy. We continued to go to the Doberman school, where, I suppose, he should have made some friends, but I was beginning to discover that Thomas was, well, antisocial. A loner. He was not a man for people and would prefer a book to a conversation. The library was his favourite place. He could not take me there so went alone, with a stack of books and I used to time his visits there. Should he not be home within two hours I would begin to howl, and, really, mammy and Mary had a hard time with me if Thomas was too long away, but I could not help my howling. This antisocial side to Thomas was a real drawback, for him if not for me. He was registered sick and was on sickness benefit, a pathetic sum that he gave to mammy. But he was a writer too, or supposed to be, and off and on he would get money for his writing. This was when the booze might make a reappearance. But not too often, because it was not too often that people wanted to buy his writing. I was about eight months old before some-one must have done, because he had been sober until then, not a spoonful, then, suddenly, it was bottle after bottle. I hated the stuff for what it did to him, that he lost all self-respect. A piss in the open, on the street, in broad daylight, meant as little to him as it did to me, and I remember once when a man complained that Thomas broke his nose. I heard the crunch of the shattered bone and a laughing, uncouth Thomas. The man was a fool to have complained, but; and this is only one incident of the many I could recount, I was beginning to understand why he had so many enemies. During the drinking, I was very alert and, as best as I could, I guarded him. Had anyone punched his nose I would have been in there biting. What else? It was in my nature and mammy knew that it was in my nature and when Thomas was finally back to himself – that he was too ill or had no money to buy more drink, she would warm him that he could lose me if he did not look out. "There are people watching you, you know." "It won't happen again." "Please God it doesn't." But I think she knew and so did I that when he regained his health and had some money the chances were it would. "What would you do if Martin was gone when you sobered up?" she asked.

"That won't happen."

"But it could."

"It won't."

Mammy said she was not so sure. "You still don't know who poisoned Martin, and whoever did that could do anything." Thomas said he had thought that she meant that I might bite someone. "That as well, or that you could get into a fight and go to jail. What would happen to Martin if you went to jail?"

Thomas said he did not know, and it did not bear to think about. But he must have thought, for it was a long time before he again drank firewater. "It would break my heart if I lost you, Martin," he told me late one night before he went to bed. "I don't know what gets into me, that I drink at all; because I know before I even start that I won't know when to stop."

Needless to say, I forgave him for it; his drinking bout, and so did mammy and Mary. I'm sure that Thomas suffered enough within himself without us taking it out on him. I couldn't anyhow, not even if I tried. The big man. And he was big okay, thick and heavy and dwarfed most other men. He did not need me as a guard, and, the guarding game, was my self- elected task. For it would have broken my heart if I lost him and the chances were I would have died, for I could not see a life without him. Mammy and Mary were okay, but Thomas was my man. The only one in the whole wide world that I gave a damn about. How good it was that he was sober, sitting on the couch with me; that, in truth, he had survived another crisis. I knew that and so did he and, from what I gathered, bad as it was, he was drinking less with me than he had before, when he had been all alone. We were finished by now with the Doberman school. The trainer told Thomas to be strict with me, and I have to say that Thomas tried. A little. He would adopt a gruff, deep, voice which I thought funny, because it was not in him to be strict with me. I obeyed what he said and when he said it for the simple reason that I wanted to please, a bit of harmony between us both. But it was never, ever, throughout the years, a master and dog sort of thing with us. He would speak to me and, "What do *you* think, Martin?" Mammy thought the Doberman School had helped us a lot. "Martin does what you tell him now." "Not before time," Mary said. "You've let that dog get away with murder." But she was fond of me, the same as mammy; if she did not like me jumping up on her, especially when my paws were muddy and she was wearing clean, new clothes. "That dog is a menace." Then after a little she would be stroking my head and feeding me a biscuit. I never jumped up on mammy, though; because I knew she was old and the weakest member of our pack and that I might knock her over.

The strange thing, at this time; when I was nearing adulthood, my whole nature seems to change and, outside the house, I was aloof and not a dog to think to pat, which I made clear by my demeanour. I would suppose this would have had some bearing on why the school trainer had instructed Thomas to be strict with me. I was, to be blunt about it, not a dog to mess with. My first winter. November and December. The long dark nights. I have forgotten to mention that we stayed in Glasgow, Scotland; where, in winter, it is a four o'clock dark and lowering skies and cold and rain and you think that it will never end. I still played with Caesar, who was careful not to nip my ears for fear I bit his nose again. And there was a new playmate called Bonzo, who was a big, brown, burly, Labrador about two years old. Bonzo's mistress was a woman named Mildred who was pulled off her feet by the bouncing Bonzo, who was as unruly a dog as I had met till then. But a friendly canine, more or less, if; in truth, he was too much for Mildred. She was tall and thin and badly stooped and not strong enough to handle Bonzo, who would have taxed a strong man. He would charge like a bull, kicking dust or grass or what; and you had to watch yourself when you were with Bonzo, that he did not bowl you over. But I have to say that I liked him, for, unlike Caesar, there was nothing mean or petty in him. He was all up front and full of life and would have faced up to a lion, never mind myself and Caesar who, compared to him, were mere pussy cats. This did not bother me at all, the exuberant Bonzo. I was pretty sure, young as I was; if it came to it that I could easily best the Labrador. Not that I thought it would come to it for, as said, he was harmless to all except for his mistress, Mildred. "That dog will be the death of me," she complained to Thomas. "I was told when he was a pup that Labradors were quiet, peaceful, animals."

I would think Mildred to have been about mammy's age, in her seventies. It was far too old to have a dog like Bonzo, and Mildred- she was at her wit's end by then- offered him to Thomas. I could not have been pals with Bonzo then, had Thomas taken up her offer. Not that there was much chance of it, but I was becoming awfully jealous, possessive, and Thomas was aware of that. There would be no two dogs in his life, not while I was there anyhow. Alec liked Bonzo's spirit. A much more open- not that that would be too hard- dog than Caesar. They were complete opposites, Caesar and Bonzo and there was no way *they* would have got along.

**

My first Christmas, not that I knew then that it was Christmas, for I was a dog, remember. But the house was festooned with decorations and we had a lighted Christmas tree against the window and I knew it was a special time. For Thomas, Mary and mammy. And if it was special for them then it was special for me, but New Year was a dangerous time for drinking. I don't know why, for it is just another day, but it seemed, from what I gathered, listening in to conversations, that Thomas had been very drunk, and drunk for days, the last New Year. "That was then and this is now," Mary said. "I don't think he'll drink." "Please be to God he doesn't." And neither did he. Not a drop over Christmas and New Year. I know he was aware of me, and, for I was now big and powerful, what might happen if he drank. Our little house. It was very much a home and we were happy and on Christmas Eve Thomas and mammy went to Midnight Mass, leaving me with Mary. After a little I began to howl as was my way, my signal out to Thomas. "Please stop it, Martin," Mary scolded, but I couldn't and I howled and howled until, finally, it became too much and she put me on my lead and took me out, into the night; it was freezing cold, in search of mammy and Thomas. It was what I thought, and true enough I soon saw them in the distance. On the street. Mammy was small and Thomas was tall and I broke away from Mary and ran to him in such a frenzy of affection that; my paws upon his chest, I almost knocked him over. The good times. They would go on for years. Mammy and Thomas and Midnight Masses. It became a ritual at Christmas time and I would be left alone with a protesting Mary, who, because of my howling, would take me out to meet them. One of the times I dragged her so that she had to run, and I was *in* the chapel. That was a laugh. For I had broken free of my lead and, going by the shrieks and screams of the first out-comers- they were not slow in turning back to in-comers - you would have thought I was a tiger. "Good boy, Martin," Thomas exclaimed, when he came out, but I knew that he was not amused. The alarmed parishioners. "God bless us and save us," one of them cried. "He broke free from his lead," Mary said. "There was nothing I could do." Thomas declared it was a storm in a teacup. "Nobody got hurt or anything." "But many a body was badly alarmed," Mary said. "It's lucky for us nobody had a heart attack — not that we know of yet, anyhow." Nobody did, as it turned out; but the following year I was kept inside for all I howled to be let outside. A *firm* Mary. She preferred to listen to my howls than to risk another such adventure.

***

Thomas thought, I think because of all the books he read, that he was smart, but the truth was he was quite a chump. For instance, I used to steal half of his breakfast and he thought it was a ghost. I would look at him, and he would look at me and I could tell he was bamboozled. His breakfast. Mammy cooked it for him and he ate it in his chair, on his lap. Beside the fire. He was a lazy thing at times, was Thomas. A big yawn before he tucked in, and it was then; when he was yawning, that I seized my chance and stole the goodies. "I'm a sausage short and one fried egg," he complained to mammy. "I just don't get it." Mammy said neither did she, and they would look one to the other and search behind chairs and under the table, looking for the thief. This took the spotlight off of me. I felt to laugh at all of this, Thomas and mammy who, for whatever reason, could not see the obvious, and thought they had a ghost.

"It's the only explanation," mammy said, "because Martin would not let anybody steal your food." Thomas agreed. "Nobody can ever catch a ghost, I don't think." I was big, wide-eyed; all innocence, this talk of a ghost, if, at first, the stealing business, I had felt a little sneaky. But not too sneaky and for not too long either and after a little it was accepted that one fried egg and one sausage would mysteriously disappear.

***

That first Christmas a tramp was arrested for sleeping inside the chapel crib, in the straw beside Maryand Joseph and the baby Jesus. Thomas thought that this was funny. "I would have done the same myself," he said, when mammy, who went to mass almost every morning, told him the story. "They didn't need to involve the police." "That's what I was thinking, but Father Murphy considered it an outrage." "What he did, calling in the cops, was more outrageous to my way of thinking." Mammy said she thought the same. "He was sleeping when the police arrived, and he must have had a rude awakening." "I'll say," Thomas said. "Father Murphy should be hanging his head in shame." I sat on the floor beside my mate, who went back to the book he had been reading. In a short time, mammy came through with the breakfast and, as ever, when he yawned and turned away, I snaffled my egg and sausage. A little later we went out. Into a cold, bright, redshot morning. "It's fucking freezing, isn't it, Martin?" Thomas was given to speak to me as though I was a human. "Jesus himself would have forgiven the tramp for sleeping in his crib."

I thought the same, but couldn't say; and we walked to our usual field where we met with Bonzo and his mistress, Mildred, who, as usual, was full of complaints in regards to her bouncing charge. "He pulls me along like I was a witch on a broomstick."

The big, brawny, tail-swishing Bonzo. He was, as ever, happy as could be. Up on his hind legs, wrestling with me. I was still growing, filling out, and he was easily the stronger. I could feel his weight, the bulk of him in our friendly, if vigourous tussle. But I had the speed, the edge to beat him, that and a sheer ferocity that I tried to hide but was rooted in my nature. Some dogs sensed this and would shy away. Even Bonzo, as wild as he was; full of exuberance, would never dare to go too far, as overstep the mark. Neither Mammy or Mary had the first idea to this other, darker, side of me, if Thomas; who was with me all the time, was beginning to suspect it. The puppy he had in his pocket when he was full of drink. Two lost, forsaken souls. The wonder was we had come together if I always thought that it was meant to be and it was only right that we were this way. In the field with Mildred and bouncing charge, our breaths like steam in the freezing day. It was the coldest I had yet known. A hoar frost thick enough to mistake for snow, which, alas, I had yet to see. I was still finding my feet, in a way; if I felt to be all grown-up. Full of life, vim and vigour; much like Bonzo, who, when we ran, would try to knock me over. It was not to be, for I was too quick, but, all bull-like rushes, he kept on trying until, at last, he was out of puff and we both lay down to rest.

After a little Thomas called for me and I jumped on him and he ruffled my head as was his habit. "You'll never guess where we are going, Martin." I hardly cared, and how could I guess anyway? Anyhow, he put on my lead; the choke chain, and we began to walk out of the field, setting a good pace. Bonzo followed a little but then turned back to re-unite with Mildred. I think, for all of his misbehaviour, that he was really fond of her. The pity was that she was just too old and frail for him and the wonder is that they had endured together for so long. A couple of years, since he was a pup; but they could not endure for too much longer. Bonzo had become too big, too much for her, who, really, when she had bought a dog should have chosen a much smaller breed. It was all one big mistake, her and Bonzo, if, as is the way with people and dogs, Bonzo would end up paying the price. No wonder I felt close to Thomas, who marched me into a police station. It was not far from the field, this station, but we had to go the long way round because of the surrounding fence. The cop behind the bar eyed me up, for I was not unknown to the local police. Indeed not, for I had once bitten one of them. But I won't go into that, not now. Thomas had some words with the cop, who was clearly astonished, and so was I, when; after an exchange of money, we were introduced to a long, thin, man who looked astonished too. The welcoming Thomas, who introduced himself as Tam. "You're coming with me," he said. The tall man declared his name was William, and that this was a big surprise to him. "I thought I was going to prison."

"You might still be going to prison," the cop told him. "He's only paid your bail for you." I did not like the look of William and my ruff went up and a long, low, growl which did not escape the cop.

"You might have been better in prison." There was an off-license over the road, across from the police station, and Thomas gave William the special paper to go inside and buy firewater. What a stupid fucking thing to do, but the whole thing was stupid, totally nuts. William was still half drunk and had straw in his hair from his stay in the crib. His night with the Holy Family. I bet *they* were glad to have seen the back of him. "We'll put him up for the night, Martin, "Thomas said. "The poor guy deserves a break."

He did? I wondered what mammy would think. And Mary. It would have been about five o'clock by now, and night was falling; closing in, and if it had been cold before it was colder now. Walking with William. He wore a black coat and had a dreadful smell and I dreaded to think how long it was since he had washed. In short, William – he had no front teeth but bragged yellow rotten side fangs – was a smelly dirty creature and I was beginning to think that the priest was right for setting the law on him. Good riddance to bad rubbish, and William would prove to be all of that, bad rubbish.

***

The night I bit the cop! It was a couple of months back, late at night in the grounds of a school where we, myself and Thomas, often went. Late at night, before we went to bed. I would run ahead of him, inside a sort of hockey pitch. It was apart from the school, but the gates were open, which; as things turned out, was too bad for the cop and almost, by dint of him, disastrous for me.

I really liked this late-night run with nobody there except for us and I had come to think we owned the place and I had taken to as guarding it. This was an innate thing, rooted in my nature, which, at the time, Thomas did not know about. No. I was full of tricks, surprises. The cop. I heard first the crackle of his radio which to me was a frightful racket, as that he had an army with him. But he was all alone. In the night. In the school. On a path above the hockey pitch. The next I knew I was up there right beside him, barking furiously. *Fuck off, whoever you are.* Thomas was like a mile behind me and if I heard him call, I paid no heed. This trespasser. I could tell that he was frightened, but it did not stop him kicking at me. A swinging boot! I dodged it easily, and when I saw the chance, I bit into his leg. A good nip that ripped his trousers and had him jump. Then Thomas was there and his hand on my collar, holding me back. The shocked, but angry man. "Does that dog belong to you?" Thomas said I did. "He's only a pup." "He's a dangerous brute," the cop told him. "He's bitten my fucking leg." Thomas said it was only a playful bite. The cop had his truncheon out by now. "I should bash his fucking head in." Thomas was crouched down, holding me back; which was quite a tussle, for I really wanted to go for that cop, who was not nearly as brave as he made out. Bash my fucking head in. He could hardly clear off fast enough, for fear that I broke free. "We haven't heard the last of this," Thomas told me when he had gone. "We'll need to deny that it was us." And that's just what we did, or Thomas did, when, some two hours later, the cop re-appeared. At our door. He was with two colleagues, and Thomas said we had been at home all night. "It must have been some other dog that bit you."

I was in the kitchen with my ear to the door while he spoke with the cops, who – in particular the one who had been bitten – were not amused. "You're a fucking liar," he snarled. "You had to pull him that cur off of me." Thomas said that he had never seen the cop in his life before. "All this is news to me." The cop was not for wearing that. "Who the fuck do you think you're kidding?"

"I'm not kidding anybody."

"You're a bare-faced liar."

"You will need to prove it"

"I've eight stitches in my leg to prove it."

"I've already told you it must have been another dog."

"It was *your* dog, you cunt."

"Mind your language," Thomas said. "It's bad enough that you come knocking on my door at this hour without the cursing." There was a scuffle at that. The outraged cop! His name was Bert, as I heard another policeman call him.

"This won't do you much good, Bert."

"I should charge him with assault," Thomas said.

"We weren't here,"

the same cop said. "You weren't at the school, and we weren't at your door. Is that alright with you, Bert?" "Whatever you say, Duncan."

Thomas said, "That's fair enough with me." And that was that. The bullying cops. Three against one, and poor Thomas with a whopper of a black eye. "That was a close shave, Martin," he told me. "If that Bert hadn't lost his temper we would have been in trouble." But Bert *had* lost his temper. "He should have been a boxer instead of a cop," Thomas said. "But I suppose a cop is second best." So it was, the bad-tempered Bert, that we; myself and Thomas, became known to the local police, who; on the whole, were not too bad and, certainly they never tried to stitch us up, to gain revenge for the bitten Bert.

***

William emerged from the off sales with a clinking bag of bottles. "Are you *really* taking me home with you?" "I said I was, didn't I?" In the night. The frozen streets. The sky was high and some first stars twinkling. We began to walk, all three of us; but not before William had a good long swig out of a wine bottle. "I needed that," he said to Thomas. "I don't know how to thank you." Thomas said nothing, and I knew; knowing him, that he was now having second thoughts. His good deed. I wondered what had come over him and I think that he did too. "We'll need to find you a place in a hostel."

"I thought that you were taking me home with you."

"I am, but only for a short time. We don't have a spare bed in my house." "I could sleep on the floor." Thomas said no. "I stay with my mother and she wouldn't have it." William swigged some more wine. "I thought you were a good guy."

Thomas said he tried to be and that mammy would make something to eat but then William would need to go. "You can sleep in a doorway or something." This did not please William, and he said as much. "I could sleep in bed with you." "You must be fucking joking."

William said nothing, which was wise of him. I could tell that Thomas was becoming fed up with it, and had I been him I would have dumped William then and there. On the street. The tall tramp. I was beginning to think he had a bit of a mental defect along with a drinking problem. But a certain sly, low, cunning which told him when to button up. Shut his mouth. Or Thomas would shut it for him. Anyhow, on we went, the three of us; and I could only wonder what mammy would say when she saw William.

"Who is *he*?"

"He's the guy who slept in the crib last night."

"I thought he was in jail."

"So he was, but I bailed him out."

"That was good of you." Mammy could be sarcastic at times. "But he can't stay here."

"He knows that, but right now he's a homeless man and it's Christmas time and I thought we could show a bit of good will."

"You did?"

"I did."

William piped up that he was not a homeless man. "I have a daughter who takes care of me." "You have?" Thomas looked to mammy who said something about the daughter not making a very good job of it. "But you could phone her up," she said to Thomas.

Thomas said he would do just that, and asked William for his daughter's number. "She can come and collect you." William hemmed and hawed about the number and said she might not come.

"You said that she takes care of you."

"We fell out."

"You can fall back in."

Mammy sat, looking disgusted. The whole affair. The drunken- he had been none too sober when Thomas had bailed him out of jail – smelly, bag of rags that had been hoisted on her. "The quicker she comes the better, "she said. By now Thomas had gotten the daughter's number out of William, who warned him, "She might want nothing to do with me." "Let's hope not." They were all sitting and I was lying on the carpet. Beside Thomas. Across from William, who was swigging at his wine bottle. It must have been a powerful brew for he suddenly said, "I could kill that dog with my bare hands." This last proved too much for Thomas who, on the moment, yanked William up by the scruff of his neck and marched him to the door. "Out," he said, "and don't come back," and I was more than pleased to hear the door slam shut on William. Mammy asked, "You didn't hit him, did you?"

"No." Thomas shook his head and a low whistle. "But maybe I should have done, because I don't think we've seen the last of him." As if on cue the front door knocked and a call from William through the letterbox. "Let me in, you fucking rotter." I began to bark, and furiously. *Let me get at him.* "Easy Martin, I can deal with this myself."

"What about the neighbours?" Mammy asked. "We can't have him shouting outside the door all night." "I'll telephone his daughter" Thomas said, and he lifted up the telephone and a short, sharp, conversation. "She says she has had enough of him, and I can't say that I blame her."

"She's still his daughter."

"She knows that, but she knows him too." By now William had begun to beg to be let back inside. "Please," he pleaded. "It's cold out here and I have a heart condition."

Mammy said we could call the law and have him locked up again. "It would be for his own good, really."

"I've only just bailed him out."

"Then more fool you, the man's a mental case."

"I know that now, but I didn't then or I wouldn't have bailed him out."

"Then put him back in." Mammy was now more than serious. "You heard what he said he would do to Martin."

"I know what I would do if he touched a hair on Martin's head."

"That's an answer to nothing," mammy answered. "We've got to get rid of him."

"But not the cops," Thomas replied, "I've never called the cops before for help and I'm not starting now."

"He's not going to just walk away," mammy snapped, "you know that the same as me."

By now, all this excitement, I was jumping up and down, wanting to get at William. Mammy repeated that we would need to get rid of him, and quickly, "Mary will soon be home." William shouted through the letterbox. "Give me a drop of wine for the love of God." Thomas said he would do that, give William wine. "And a little something else as well." At this particular time Thomas was having trouble with his sleeping and, as a result, as a temporary cure, the doctor had prescribed him Nembutal. A couple of them and he was out in no time. It was an ideal way, if a stronger dose; the powder out of three or four capsules – they were a bright yellow cooler – mixed in with wine, to shut up William. "He'll sleep for a long time when he gets that down him." Mammy was a bit dubious at this drastic measure. "He said he had a bad heart, and we don't want to kill him." "But we want to get rid of him, don't we?" Mammy agreed. What else? I think she was frightened that Thomas might go out and thump William. "But we still don't want to kill him." "He's only in for a long sleep." With that Thomas locked me in the kitchen and then I heard him opening the front door. I cocked my ears to try and hear what they were saying and heard William thanking Thomas in a whiny voice. "Good on you, I'm in bad need of this."

At that we, all three of us, retired to the living room. I was still hopping mad, but; somehow, realized that I had seen the back of William. Thomas rolled a cigarette, and mammy said, "Thank God you're sober." Thomas said that it was William who should be thanking God that he was sober.

Outside the door William was singing, *Oh Danny boy, the pipes the pipes are calling, from glen to glen and ...then* his voice began to fade and waver and the next we heard was loud snoring. "That took less time than I thought it would," Thomas laughed. He looked at his watch. "About fifteen minutes."

"But we have to get rid of him." mammy said.

"We will, don't worry about that." Thomas sat calmly smoking, looking sombre. "I'll put him back inside the crib."

"Do you think you'll be able to carry him, he'll be a dead weight?"

"I don't have much option but to try, do I?"

"He can't weigh too much; he's as thin as a rake, isn't he?"

I sat low growling, listening in to this conversation. Thomas and mammy, and I knew full well there was something afoot concerning the unpleasant William. He had said he was going to kill me. Some hope. He was sleeping now because of it. Thomas finished his smoke and told Mammy that he might as well do it now, remove the snoring William. "The chances are that people will think he's drunk." Mammy commented that he should try and be discreet. "Especially when you put him back inside the nativity crib." "I will." Thomas put on his coat and hat and patted my head. "I won't be too long Martin."

And neither he was. I would think about ten or fifteen minutes. "Did you get on alright?" mammy asked. "I've got a bit of a sore back," Thomas answered. "He was out to the world and heavier than I thought he'd be." Mammy asked if we should phone the priest about the tramp being back inside the crib, but Thomas said we'd better not. "They might twig he's drugged and put the blame on me. I mean, I bailed him out, didn't I? I've covered him with straw behind the three Wise men and it's better that he stays there till morning." There were times and this was one when mammy had to lean on Thomas, his judgment. A massive dose of Nembutal. "I hope he makes it through the night." Thomas said he was sure he would. "But I don't want to see his ugly mug again."

"He might remember where we live."

"I don't think so. It was dark and he was drunk. He might not even remember that he was in jail. He'll be all befuddled when he wakes up. But one thing's for sure, he'll have a good sleep if nothing else." I was more contented now that things were back to normal. The cold winter night and our twinkling Christmas tree, and it was time for my evening meal. It was usually a dried food mixed with water with, if I was lucky, some sardines stirred through it. A wholesome diet, and plenty of it; one good feed a day, if; as I would discover as the years passed by, I would be fed tinned food as a Christmas treat.

Chappie or Chum or Pal or some such name. The problem was that I much preferred the former. The dried dog food, and it was a huge frustration that I could not say, tell them. This is one of the crosses which are the lot of a dog, that he cannot tell his preferences. Thomas and mammy imagined I much preferred the brand name food when the truth was the opposite. I was a bit upset for Thomas that his good turn, if it was as daft a thing as he had done till then, had ended in disaster. The abusive William. He was back in the crib when, once again, due to the vigilant priest, he would be re-arrested and, he must have thought that it was all a dream, his time with us, we never heard from him again.

***

By now I had a couple more doggy friends that I would meet with at night in the hockey field beside the school. I think Thomas enjoyed a talk with their masters and I enjoyed a play with them. A couple of mongrels, Bruce and Bob who, Bob, was a tiny little thing with a whiskered face which was not unlike a rat's. He was something of a biter, which was encouraged by his master, who was a big fat man named Snowy, on account of having a head of pure white hair. He had a loud, booming laugh and was a bit of a bully-boy himself. When, that is, much like his dog, the whiskered Bob, he thought to get away with it, so it was on the cards that we would clash, myself with Bob and Thomas with Snowy. Bruce was altogether a different sort and so was his master, a man called Henry. Both of them were civil and well meaning. Needless to say, they were under the heel of Bob and Snowy. Their night time walks in the hockey pitch. They had been there for a long time before we came, and Bob soon made clear I was not welcome. He was a game, cocky little guy, I'll say that for him. How he tried to as chase me away. Out of the school, the hockey pitch. This of course delighted Snowy. "He'd stand up to a lion, Bob would." For my part, I did not want to hurt the little dog, who, in a way, was acting up only to please his master. The big, fat, loud mouthed – you could hear him before you saw him – Snowy, "A man like him should have a big, fierce dog," Thomas said, "not that little rat-faced Bob." I agreed with a couple of woofs. Dogs and men, they can become alike; as, by now I was becoming to be like Thomas. Somewhat aloof and something of a loner. For instance, while it was fun to play with other dogs I could as easily do without them, and one sure thing I could have done without the rat-faced Bob. He was a pain in the arse, his growling at me. I tried to ignore him, but that only made him bolder, and, I knew, knowing him, that Thomas thought I should put an end to it. This was fair enough with me, but I was too slow; or Thomas was – I could read him like a book by now, and what to do to please him – because, right out of the blue, Bruce turned on Bob and ran him out of the pitch and into the school grounds and out into the streets and that was the end of him and his bullying ways.

We came on the scene minutes after to witness a heated argument between Snowy and Henry. Two men and their two dogs. It happens. Snowy was far from pleased about what had happened. The cowardly Bob, and he to take it out on the normally placid Henry. What a mistake! Snowy got in the first punch, a right to Henry's head, but that was all. Henry like a whirlwind. We were to learn later that he had been a boxer in his youth, and, a left and right, he laid out Snowy who, when he was fit to walk or stagger away, never returned to the field again. Not him or the whiskered Bob.

Henry was a bit embarrassed by his show of fisticuffs. "That was the first I've thrown a punch in forty years or even more." Thomas said he should forget it. "He punched you first, after all." "I know he did, but I'm still all shook up'" Henry wiped his forehead with a white handkerchief. "I didn't think Bruce had it in him, to set about Bob the way he did." We would be friends, all four of us; myself and Bruce and Thomas and Henry, for years to come. Our night time walks. A talkative Henry who amused Thomas with stories of his time in India, in the army where he had learned to box. This was before the war, in 1939. "It was a good time, before the fighting all begun." When the fighting did begin was transferred to Egypt and then North Africa, where he had been captured by the Germans. "I was a p.o.w for the next three years."

"Half of the time he exaggerates," Thomas said, "but I like his stories anyhow." For my part I liked my runs in the hockey pitch and so I was glad he liked the stories. Time in time and little things and my life was good, better than; when I was a pup on the fetid mattress, I could have dreamed that it would ever be.

***

In the second half of January Thomas began to drink. I don't know why, and I don't think he did either. But an unquenchable thirst. Bottle after bottle. It had begun with beer and whisky and went on to wine and rough, cheap, cider. Anything, as his money went, to keep it going, to prolong the binge which, as usual, soon led to trouble. A couple of fights – he lost a tooth in one of them - and I hated it as much or even more than Mammy, and I was really pleased when he had no more wherewithal. "I must be nuts," he told me when he had sobered up. "Because I know how it will end before I start to drink." I licked his face and wagged my tail, for I was overjoyed that he had regained his sanity. That we'd be out and about, in the fields again. A man and his dog and the man in control. The other way, when he was drunk, was upside down and I hated it. A sense of unease. Uncertainty. Mammy had had to feed me. The drunken Thomas. He had been unable to look after himself, so how could he care for me? Mammy and Mary did their best, as stood by me, but it was not the same without him. I was his dog and we all knew that and I could only wait and hope that he recovered.

***

On the doggy front, this return to normality, I was meeting again with Duke and Bonzo, who, Bonzo, was every bit as wild as ever, and, it caused me a shiver, when Mildred told Thomas that she thought to have him neutered. "It would make him less aggressive, I have been told." Thomas said that rather than aggressive Bonzo was happy and high spirited. "There's not a mean bone in his body." These humans, they could do what they wanted with our kind: mutilate and castrate us and we had no say. None at all, for should we rebel they could, as lambs to the slaughter, have us put down. Any trumped-up charge was good enough, and the vets seemed to be more than willing. An exchange of the wherewithal, or, sometimes, if the master was too mean for that, we could be dumped from cars on to open roads that were miles from anywhere. I had seen my sister kicked to death, but until now; in my time with Thomas, had forgotten their awful power. The Bonzo business brought it home again in no uncertain fashion. The lot of a dog. I was protected by Thomas, and Thomas alone, who, such irony, his addiction to the bottle, was in need of protection himself at times. But he was sober now and made it clear that he did not agree with Mildred. "Bonzo should live his life the way he is, or you should find another home for him."

"That's not what the vet told me."

"The vet only wants money."

"He's driving me crazy," Mildred said, "the way he is."

"You've put up with it this long, what's another year or two – you can see how happy he is and this problem will surely go away when he is older." Mildred said she did not know. "I'm not fit for a dog like Bonzo, not the way he is right now." Bonzo was oddly subdued, this talk about him, if he should retain his manhood, or part with it in the hope he became more docile, easy to handle. At this point, fate or what, Bonzo spied a cat outside the field, on the road, and, as was his wont, went haring out after it - straight through the same space in the railings as where Sabre had gone - and came to grief under the wheels of a motor car. Poor Bonzo. He did not deserve to die like that and I was very upset and so was Thomas and Alec, and Mildred was in tears, *her* Bonzo. He had been one fine dog, if a little wild and more than impulsive, which, in the end, his impulsiveness, had been the death of him.

As for Duke, he hardly cared and was; I'm sure, glad to see the back of Bonzo who had been besting him in all their play, knocking him down and whatnot. One sure thing, Alec would not; not for aggressiveness, ever need to think to castrate Duke, for he was one big phony who was good for a snarl, but nothing else. Or maybe a sneak bite at another, smaller, weaker dog, for he was a cagey one, was Duke. There was little chance of him out in the road, and all the rushing traffic. One could do worse than to take a leaf out of Duke's book, for a lesson in survival. We, myself and Thomas, went out of the field and – for Bonzo was still alive but all smashed up and bleeding from the mouth – did we did not look back, for it was all too sad, the smashed up Bonzo. "He had one big heart," Thomas said, "I'll say that for him."

For the rest of the day and into the night I could sense my big mate's sadness. A sort of melancholia. He pretended to be reading a book, but that was all, pretended. There was a soft, compassionate side to Thomas that he tried to hide away. "You sometimes wonder what it's all about, don't you, Martin?" We were in our room and sitting on my couch. The put-out Thomas. The Bonzo business had been a blow, but I was becoming used to it, dead dogs. My sister, then Sabre, now Bonzo. Thomas of course knew nothing about my sister, which was just as well for my old master. He was such a brute but he had been a coward when it had come to a clash with Thomas. God only knows what would have happened if he had found out about my sister. I would have wanted my old master to have a broken nose at the very least. This was a *thing* about Thomas that I had come to notice, pick up on, that he had a weakness for the vulnerable, the undefended. It was no bad thing and it was good for me, especially when I had been a puppy and he could have seen the back of me. "That road's a fucking menace, Martin." I had to agree by giving a growl. Thomas in a queer blue mood, the poor departed Bonzo. "He was full of life, just like you." But I am *yours*, and I licked his face tell him so. "Bonzo would not have cared if *you* had died because he did not belong to you," It was what I would have said if I could talk in the attempt to uplift my master. Or guardian. I was beginning to think of him more as my guardian than a master. In truth, he had never been my master, more; all in all, that we were equals if, at times, for the sake of safety, I had to follow his commands and do the things he said. It was no hardship, obeying him and I liked to please, anyhow. I would not think to run across a road as Bonzo had. Mildred could not call him back, the disobedient Labrador. Had they gone to some dog training school Bonzo might still be alive. It would, certainly, a training school, have been worth a try before thinking of castrating him.

***

Where we stayed was pretty wild, with gangs of youths who would sometimes fight with one another. These fights would often take place beside the school, where there was lots of waste ground which was sometimes used for playing football. I disliked the youths, and they disliked me. No wonder. I was forever growling at them, since, when he had been drunk, Thomas had fallen down and they had tried to rob him of a bag of booze. I had sat on his chest and bared my teeth and easily frightened them away. Ever since then they had hated me and I had hated them and Thomas, for his part, this open hostility, put two and two together and could only side with me. "But I don't want you to bite them, Martin." There was little chance of that, for they were none too brave and gave us a wide berth. *Batman and Robin.* It was what they called us and the names – for we were classed as a single unit – stuck to us for many years. Different youths and different gangs and their giggling, stupid girlfriends, who, I think, urged on the boys to fight with one other. For a season or two, at a certain age, and then they would disappear to be replaced by a different mob, and mobs. But our name remained, if I don't know who was who if I suspect that Thomas was Batman and I was Robin. It hardly matters, and after a while they accepted us and we accepted them.

A more sinister feature, in the field inside the school grounds was a man who peddled drugs. His name was Alfie and he had two white Staffordshire Bull Terriers. Thomas and I avoided him, and them. We wished no trouble, if; I have to say, the youths were silly enough without the help of Alfie and his drugs. Such, in short, gangs and drugs and some knifings and a murder – the murder was something to do with the drugs- was where we lived, and you had to have your wits about you. I mention, the drugs and Alfie, because on the night of the day of Bonzo's passing Thomas had a row with him. I don't know what it was about, for, as said, we usually avoided him and his dogs. But not that night. Thomas was hardly in a mood for avoiding him or anyone else and following some angry words he punched Alfie on the mouth. This brought a reaction from his dogs, one of whom leapt up onto Thomas's thigh in an attempt to savage him, and I mean savage, before I stepped in. A grip of the dog by the scruff of his neck as though it was a rat. I was filled with rage and had twice my normal strength and I tossed him in the air. In the night, in the field; which was hard with frost under a big bright yellow moon. When I dropped him down, he had no fight left and ran away, followed by his mate. They were not so tough, those Staffordshires; and neither, going by the looks of things, was their master, Alfie. One punch on the mouth was enough for him and he was out of the field as quickly as his dogs, or almost. I stood side by side with Thomas, who was clutching his thigh and still angry. "That fucking Alfie asked me to help him sell his drugs." We walked for a bit and then went home, and after Thomas had washed the blood from his thigh, went to bed. Next morning to my delight he was back to his usual self and when he turned his head, I was not slow in stealing half of his breakfast.

***

I turned one year old the following month, in March of 1984. A long time for a dog, it's short life in earthly terms, but nothing in the cosmic. No, not a blink. As I am telling this story Thomas has long thought me dead, but I am still here; and closer to him now than then. That aside, and think what you will – whatever takes your fancy – one year old is a good age for a dog. We are full of life, vim and vigour and, for myself, as happy as could be. A sense of security, of belonging. Our little family. Thomas and Mammy and Mary and me. Martin. I was used to my name by now, or, as Mammy still referred to me, *the wee dog*. She must have needed an eyesight test, for I was far from a wee dog when I was one year old. A bit on the rangy, coltish side but far from wee. I would never be tall, but I was thick in the chest and shoulders and altogether sturdier than the taller, more rangy Doberman. They always struck me as far too thin, all the look of a greyhound, some of them; and the same long pointed muzzle. Mine was much more blunt and short and made for a much stronger bite. I would, as I aged, go on to weigh some ninety pounds, but Mammy would still call me wee. What matter? She had helped me out when I *was* wee, all big black eyes and clinging on to the drunken Thomas. Nobody else called me that, wee, and had someone heard her call me that when I was one year old, the chances were they would have thought her nuts. A wee dog. What they didn't know I was very much the baby of the family. The one to look out for, if, how things went, it was sometimes me who was looking after Thomas.

***

The field was not the same without Bonzo. We still had Alec and Duke, and even Mildred re-appeared with a new dog, a small cross-breed named Toby. She had acquired him from the dog rescue and he had a scruffy badly treated look and was nervous and withdrawn. A far cry from the exuberant Bonzo, but, all in all, much more suited to her. Changing times. A new year. 1984. It was but a number and meant nothing to us. But I think to mention in the interest of chronology. Earthly time, my time with Thomas. When I was a bouncy, happy, one year old. It is a wonderful age if you are a dog. Things are still all new and you are not a puppy any more, and I had discovered that I was gay. This was an affront to Thomas who prided himself for his manliness, masculinity, and, I think, feared that we might both be tarred with the same brush. "I wish that you would stop it, Martin," he would complain whenever I tried to mount another dog. "You'll get a name about you." I already had a name. All the dogs I knew, including Duke, who now sat down quickly when I came near, would shun away at the sight of me. Thomas tried to laugh it off, but I knew he was far from pleased. "A boy dog should fancy a girl dog." Not me, no sir. I was what I was and there was nothing I could do about it. Not that I was over-sexed, if, occasionally, I would get a sudden urge and be right in there, not giving a damn for anyone, including Thomas who was honestly shocked that I was gay and nothing he could do about it. My big mate. He had not the heart to de-ball me and, in a way, my inclination helped to make me top-dog in the neighbourhood. Thomas was far from proud of this, given how, in part at least, I had achieved my domination. That; some quirk, twist, he had to have a gay dog. He tried not to make a big thing of it, and neither will I. More a mention in the passing. What I was. Thomas was the opposite. One for the ladies when, that was, he got lucky. I have to say that it was damn rarely. We are speaking here of a middle-aged man who had only me. His best pal. I was his only pal, when I come to think about it.

***

He had a religious bent, had my big mate; and in the spring of that year he, or we, began to attend a Tuesday night novena to St Anthony in St Francis Chapel in the Gorbals. The chapel was a forty-minute walk from where we lived, and Mary would come with us. You had to complete nine consecutive Tuesdays for a full novena, which was okay with me. The walk to the chapel and back again, and I began to know when it was Tuesday. Don't ask me how – some subconscious clock? - but I knew it was a Tuesday night long before Thomas said, "St Anthony's, Martin." Off we would go, all three of us and me on my lead, the choke chain. Not that I needed it by then, but I was used to it and so was Thomas. We would, if we did not know it at that time – how could we? – use the same chain for the next nine years. Some five full novenas. Inside the chapel we would sit at the back and I was wise enough to be on my best behaviour. A good dog. I'll say I was. You could have sat me on a mantelpiece like some stuffed owl for all the noise I made. I was none too sure that Thomas prayed, but I knew he liked the atmosphere. People who were trying to be good. It must have made a change from the dives he had frequented. As for me it was all a mystery, and I was the only dog in the chapel. St Francis was a huge building in Cumberland Street, not far from where they, Thomas and Mary, had grown up. I heard them speak about it sometimes, a much different place – the present one was a neat a suburb – where it had been all gas-lit streets and tenements and they had been poor and their electric light had been cut off. "Do you remember we had to ask the priest for candles?" Mary said she did. "The house was all shadowy and dead ghostly." Thomas said he had been dead scared, but I couldn't imagine him being scared. The novena began at eight and we were out at nine, sometimes sooner. This was a whole new side to Thomas, the religious aspect. But he was full of surprises and even surprised himself at times, buying me for instance. He had certainly surprised a many other people who had thought for him to kick me out when he had sobered up. They had been in for a disappointment when day after day I still was there, if I almost went when I was poisoned. A nursing Thomas and his feeding me with a dummy teat. Still, it had been no bad thing, not really; for we had then forged our tie completely then. An almighty bond that would survive the years and my big mates try for women. He was always on the lookout, I can tell you that. For a shapely leg or a nice plump arse. I don't think he could help himself, and I would catch him gawking when – I think it was a good place for it, eyeing up the ladies – we were in the chapel. The Tuesday night Novena.

Thomas was smarter than usual, all washed and shaved and full of lust and, certainly, he saw nothing wrong in fornication. Nor did I, not then; my life as a dog, if I was always jealous and a little frightened that a woman might drive a wedge between us. Thomas's faults. He had more than a few, and so had I for that matter. Indeed, in a way, I was worse than him, for, had I my way, had he approved, I would have been a rapist. As it was, I had risked his wrath with other dogs; all of them male, on many an occasion. A distraught Thomas. "What the fuck is the matter with you, Martin?" I would hand my head as if in shame, and I suppose I was, in a way, for upsetting my big mate. But that is the way it had to be, earthly pleasures; flesh and blood, and we were a pair of brutes to tell the truth, if Thomas would deny it. The way he was, still is; and, for he is older now, he thanks God for Viagra. There was no need for pills for him back then, in the eighties. The nine consecutive Tuesdays. You got to know the congregation and, I'm sure, with some of them, Thomas more than casually, for he would be out all night, which, was a huge vexation.

**

It is confusing, I know; this narrative, for, for a dog, I knew too much as I am sure you are aware. But consider me, the task I have in relating this, my time on earth, for I was a dog and nothing more, when I was with Thomas.

A DOG'S OWN STORY

***

Alec was out of school and had a job by now and we were not seeing too much of him and Duke. Not that I cared too much. Duke had always been surly and not much of a playmate. That and, of late, in our last few meetings, he would hardly get off of his bum. This caused Thomas a rather coarse laugh. "I think people are getting to wise up to you now, Martin." He would speak to me, like I was human. A man much like himself, except, that is, in our sexual tastes. Still and all he was coming to accept what I was and at times I think he thought it funny. Duke, for instance, would sit pitifully and look at Alec, who, Alec, thought it anything but funny and began to go out of his way to swerve us. Anyhow, we seldom saw them, Duke and Alec or, for that matter, any other cared-for dog and his protective, outraged owner. My rough ways. It was different when I met with bitches, who viewed me with distaste; an utter contempt. So it was that I had no friends, and it would continue like that with one exception all my earthly years. A short span, if – and what is a long time, for Methuselah came and went and the world went on – at that time, when I was young and full of life and I thought that it would last forever. With Thomas. As that we were two immortals cheating time rather than the mortal misfits that we were. For no mistake, my mate and me, for all he liked the ladies – about the only normal thing about him – we did not fit in amongst our fellows. I was a pariah in the dog world and he had not a single friend amongst the humans. Two weirdoes and the good thing was we had each other. Birds of a feather and all of that. A normal dog would not have suited Thomas.

It was the unusual that appealed to him, the William thing and stuff like; like the night I bite the policeman.

Around this time, the novena nights; a carnival set up in the field and there were some vicious dogs, big wolf-like half-starved creatures that were up for a fight and I had a run-in with one of them. A monster who was twice my size, but he was much too slow and I emerged an easy winner. This did not please his master and there was a scuffle of sorts between him and Thomas, who, too, emerged an easy winner, without a scratch. "But I don't like to see you fighting, Martin."

So, we avoided the field and the big wild dogs and began to go to a nearby park instead. There were lots of dogs and humans there, but they mostly kept away from us. Eventually though, how such things go, I made the acquaintance of a Boxer dog who was too old and decrepit – heavens above, he was falling apart – to interest me in any way other than companionship. This dog went by the name of Spud and it turned out that Thomas knew his mistress, who worked in a local betting shop. She was a blonde-haired brassy looking bitch who, her name was Fidelma, played up to him and, "I want to fuck her," he told me, "And I think I will, just wait and see." What else? I could hardly run away, could I? Wait and see and *hear*. Thomas and Fidelma. In a room in her house, in the afternoon. Myself and Spud were outside listening, their humphing, and the wonder was that the bed stood up to their abuse. We looked one to the other in disgust. Or, to be more precise, I looked at Spud in disgust. His mistress. She was a married woman if such a trifle hardly bothered Thomas. He was not a man to care too much about a husband. Nor was she by the sound of things, for they were right in there and that's a fact. This *fornication*. When they came out from the room they kissed a bit before, thank God, we left the house and out to the clean, fresh, open air.

***

This state of affairs went on for months, almost daily, until Fidelma had to move abroad, with her husband – what a chump he was, had been. For myself I was delighted, if my big pal felt the opposite. "I will miss her, Martin." I licked his hand to comfort him, that at least he still had me. A faithful companion, and I forgave him of course. He was down in the mouth for a couple of weeks, and it was as well he did not know of my glee. How happy I was that it was over, that once more, we only had each other. A man and his dog. It was the impression we gave, and a true one too, if, from the very first, there was always something else. Anyhow, by now; after Fidelma went, the carnival had long gone from the field and it was safe to return and we met again with Alec and Duke, who were not very pleased to see us. Alec thought Duke should stand up for himself while Duke thought it safer to just sit down. "He's not like this with any other dog, only Martin." Thomas said he wondered why and Alec pretended not to know, the better to not offend him. It was much easier just to leave the field, to avoid us once again. Not that I was caring. I had Thomas back again and that was all that mattered.

***

Suzie was a German shepherd who was pretty enough if you were into bitches. All black and gold and alert brown eyes and a luscious, sweeping tail. I was a little jealous of her tail given my short, docked one. That and I was a little leery of her, if not downright frightened to begin with; until, that was, I began to get to know her. My sweet Suzie. There was no badness in her, none at all and she took to me in a way that male dogs couldn't. There was always the threat of a fight with them, however veiled. Not so with Suzie, and we became good friends and equals. I would never have thought to try and bully her who, if it came to it, could hold her own in any doggy company. There was nothing meek about this girl who was in her prime, about two years old. A proud hussy. From pure bred stock. You could tell that by her bearing. Proud and haughty except, that was, when her master smacked her on the nose with a rolled-up newspaper. He was a tall, thin, ex-policeman who believed that this, a hit on the nose with a newspaper, was the best thing for obedience, that Suzie did as she was told. I could have told him otherwise, that he was only shaming her in front of me, and, bit by bit, with each blow of the rolled-up newspaper, reducing her proud spirit.

While I detested this creature, his treatment of Suzie, I have to admit that I was glad that he was a man. The loathsome Fidelma who had smelled quite rank, unpleasant to me. Poor old Spud, stuck with her, wherever she was. I hoped far, far away from myself and Thomas, who needless only to say, still missed his floozie and their afternoons together. While I played quite happily with Suzie, I was always aware of her thin, ex-policeman master. He would, it seemed to me, strike her on a whim, his rolled-up newspaper, and, in result, she was reduced to whimpering. "A fucking bully," Thomas said, and I knew he felt like chinning the master, but had he done that then Suzie would have turned on him and I would have gone for Suzie. It was a hopeless, no-win situation and we could only walk away before things, and bad as they were for the hapless Suzie, got really out of hand. This is the sad thing is that a dog like her will lay down her life for a worthless, no-good master. So, in short order, for Thomas could not abide the master, I would think two weeks or even less, I lost the only bitch I ever liked and who in turn had liked me. However, as a sort of solace – did Thomas know that I missed Suzie? – it was soon time for a holiday.

***

It was my first time in the city centre, and people edged away from us. A slight alarm? Thomas was big and so was I and it can't be too often for a pair like us to be in the city centre, in the railway station. Our holiday. I had no idea where we were going, but wherever it was I did not care as long as we were together. On the train I sat on the floor, as a good dog should; and I was trying hard to be just that, a good dog. The wish to please. Our adventure. I was not about to spoil it by growling at some stranger.

We alighted from the train at Girvan, which is a town on the Ayrshire coast. That's what Thomas told me anyhow when we were walking from the station. In a fine, clear, blue-skyed day. "We are staying in a caravan in a place named Byne Hill," he said. It was a fair walk out of town – it appeared to have only one main street – to Byne Hill and after a little we paused for a picnic, and I had a special treat. A tin of Chappie. I was usually fed a sort of dried dog food that was mixed with little fishes that were tasty enough and encouraged me to eat all the food. The Chappie made for a pleasant change and - Thomas had not forgotten my two bowls, one for food and the other for water –I wolfed it down. Thomas sat on a rock and ate homemade sandwiches and drank a flask of coffee. "It's good up here, isn't it, Martin?" I licked his face in agreement. "I used to want to become a boxer, and this place would have made a great training camp," he said. "Maybe if I had had you back then I *would* have become a boxer."

After our picnic we were off again, to find our caravan on Byne Hill. A bit of exploring. The country life. It was a feeling of freedom to be away from the city and the people who did not like us. I was always afraid that they might maim or murder Thomas. Someone had tried to poison me to get at him, remember. The poisoning in the garden. It was a constant fear anyhow, and I was always on my guard for him; and especially so if he took drink. On Byne Hill. There was a sort of path between the fields and looking down you could see the sea and after a short time we came to a grassy meadow which was full of wild, white, daisies and almost dead centre of the meadow stood a small lone caravan, and, "That is it, I think," Thomas said. "The caravan I booked."

***

Running. On the hard wet sand near the water's edge and the feeling that I could run forever. A surging power. I went way out in front of Thomas before turning back to ensure that he was still there. On the beach and we were all alone, the two of us, in a red-shot, balmy night. The spray from the sea and my head in the air and Thomas would throw a stick into the water for me to wade out and retrieve it. Or so he thought, but I was no sea-dog and had no intention of becoming one. Let him go out and fetch the stick and I would have followed after. It was always that way, following him. All the time, from the very start, from the moment when I had climbed onto the back of his hand and clung there and would not let go. A mystical, almost magical trip and lots of adventures still to come.

This pretence I was a normal dog when all the time, in the root of me, I knew I was something else. Not that I cared too much, more a dim, if persistent nag that I could not put my paw on, and, anyhow, I was content to be just who I was, a dog named Martin. With my big mate, who had already been through a lot with me. The night I bit the policeman. He had taken a vicious punch to get us out of that one. A huge black eye. But he had laughed it off and joked that the cop should have been a boxer. Then we had William, the haughty tramp who had enraged Thomas by threatening to kill me with his bare hands. He had been sorted out by the Nembutal mixed in with his wine. A sound sleep! In the Christmas crib where he had been dumped and, thankfully, that was the last that we had seen of him. Then, and I would think his biggest woe, was the sex business, my mounting other males, which, if I could not refrain from doing so, had caused him great embarrassment. All this and more, my howling when he was not there – except, that is, in Fidelma's house where I knew where he was and knew I should keep quiet. Both myself and Spud, who, I think, was used to it, Fidelma's infidelities, I could barely believe my luck when she had moved away, if Thomas thought that it a great misfortune. But only for a little while, as he had a fickle heart and soon was bouncing back. A man of resilience, I'll say that for him. That he had lived this long was a testament to that. A lot of luck and a survival harp which, given that he had fostered me, was just as well for both of us.

***

The caravan had steep wooden steps, leading to the door. Not that I ever thought to use them. One leap and I was inside. Our new home. I was very much a one-man dog, and I can't say that I missed Mammy or Mary, who, probably, both of them, would be glad to have a rest from us. *Batman and Robin*. We had become well known in the neighbourhood, especially among the local cops, who, I have to say, appeared to bear no grudges. We were never hassled, and it would have been easy for them to have hassled us. I was a dangerous dog and all of that. But they had let it go, after, that is, the assault on Thomas. His black eye. It was small penance for a savaged leg and we were not complaining. The inside of the caravan was surprisingly spacious, well laid- out. We had a toilet and bedroom and a dining area and living room that was complete with a table and chairs and a long, low, couch where I would sit while Thomas sat at the table and tried to write. I'd fancy this the reason for our holiday, that he got

64

down to writing. Not that it had done him much good till now, the long hours he spent writing. As I have said before he had next to nothing and it was usual for him to borrow from Mary to buy his cigarette tobacco. Off and on he would sell a story, and after he had to pay her back the rest of the money went on drink. We all hated it when this occurred and I would think we were more than fortunate that, for all his efforts, he did not sell too many stories. Thomas would work at night. A couple of hours. Smoking and drinking coffee. Then it was off to bed, together. A rare closeness. He would have a final smoke and then put out the light. "Goodnight, Martin." So it went, our holiday. A long one. I would think three weeks or even more. Seaside walks and walking into Girvan to stock up on food and tins of Chappie. I was eating, easily, two large tins a day and it was no wonder that at home I was fed the dried food stuff. We went together about twice a week to buy it, the dried dog food. A brand named Wilson's! This food was exclusive to pet shops and there were always dogs inside the place – we met Alec and Duke a few times there – and the assistant would shovel the stuff out of a huge sack onto a scale to weigh it. I have no idea how much it cost, except, I'm sure, it was a fraction of the price of Chappie. There were no pet shops in Girvan, so Thomas had to fork out for my Chappie. A tin in the morning and another at night. At home I was fed only once a day, so it was better than good the time we spent on holiday, on Byne Hill; where we had found a secluded path that led down to the sea and a walk straight into town. The shop that sold the Chappie. This, when we were in town, was the only time that I was on a leash, so that I would not frighten anybody. This is a problem for the bigger dog, no matter how gentle, that they can frighten humans. So, I had to be leashed for appearance's sake if nothing else when we were amongst them. Not that I minded and I think I knew; had picked up on it, that Thomas would put the lead on me wherever humans were about, which was wise, for, quite simply, I was not a dog for a stranger's pat. Far better I was left alone for I was always afraid that I might be stolen, daft as that might sound.

Idyllic days. Sweet interlude. Running on the sand. Sometimes Thomas would run with me, but he could not keep up and; for I delighted in this running, I was soon way out in front again. But who was caring, certainly not us. It was all a fun thing, and we would sometimes box, like dummy fight, on the beach where, if you saw us, you might have thought it was for real. Something like our day in the park when Thomas had taken a paw in the eye. He had no intention of that again and was quick to stop it when he thought things were getting out of hand, as they might well have done in the heat of the action. On the sand. I was about as tall as him when I stood on my hind legs and had huge sharp teeth and it would have been easy to have been carried away and, in that state, for something dreadful to have happened. It was really a stupid, dangerous play and Thomas should have had more sense than to have encouraged it. Our boxing. I was supposed to be Big Boy Peterson and he was Joe Louis. It made a from Batman and Robin, but it was really daft to say the least – if Joe Louis was rushed to hospital.

***

Mammy and Mary were glad to see us, safe and sound. There was always the worry, especially with Mammy, that Thomas would drink and, afterwards, suffer some disaster. That he might even lose me if things turned really sour. There was always that possibility and she knew what it would do to him when he sobered up. "Where's Martin?" "He got run over when you were drunk." I could well imagine the distraught Thomas. *Me*. Big Boy Peterson, his best pal, under a truck or bus. It would have all but have destroyed him, and she knew that and, in result, worried more about the drinking than she had ever done before. Thomas and the wee dog. We had become as one, and, as such, were dependant on each other. Due to this dependency, he had cut down on his drinking. Had he continued to drink the way he had before I came, he would have had no chance of keeping me and I did my best to keep him sober. In the world. Glasgow is a pretty tough city for such an aggressive drunk as he was. That and he was becoming older, slower, much less alert than he had once been. Let's just say that he was too old – Joe Louis was washed up in his thirties – for the rough and tumble of street fighting. But tell him that, as, I'm sure, some people told Joe Louis before he was almost killed by Rocky Marciano. In Thomas's case the chances were more for a knife in the back or in his neck. Not that it worried him, this danger, and it was only when I came along that he began to treat booze with the respect that it deserved. But all the time, and from a very young age, it had been a cross for him to carry. There was no such thing as a social drink or even a one - night drunken spree. It was the whole hog for him should he take a sip of alcohol.

Something in his make-up. The urge for more and more and the more he drank it was as a demon taking over. There was only one way out for him, and that was not to drink at all and- for he knew that – there were long sober spells, nine months or a year before he slipped and drank again and it was as bad or worse than it had been before.

***

We started the firm, *Doberman Securities*, shortly after our return from Girvan. "We need to make some money, Martin." We did? Well, if he said so. The wherewithal that was the name of the game amongst the humans. "Besides, I can still do my writing while we are guarding places." He could? But the problem was to find a place for us to guard. We had a couple of interviews with male humans who sat behind big desks. "Look fierce, Martin." I gave a growl or two; enough, I'd warrant, to alarm the humans, but the interviews came to nothing. *Doberman Securities*. It was only me and him and, I think, they had been expecting a little more than that. A gang of sorts, humans and dogs. But we had no gang and would never have one. Thomas tried his best, adverts and such, but we had no luck until an unlikely woman stepped in. Her name was Mrs. Smart, and I felt a withering in my heart the moment I first saw her. A shrew of a creature dressed in a dark business suit and showing off her legs. Thomas seemed beguiled by her, who – I could tell by her smell, my doggy nose – was far from young if she tried her best to disguise the fact. A made-up face and her hair was a dyed blond and she had long, blood red fingernails. I could sense, straight from the start; the instant she set eyes on him, that she fancied Thomas. This wizened tart. Such a brazen flirt, the way she looked; a smile, to him who was looking for work and not romance, not initially anyhow. Mrs. Smart explained, much like our other would- be employers had, that she had assumed that Doberman Securities consisted of more than just myself and him, and that should have been the end of it. Another knockback, but Mrs. Smart was not for letting Thomas go so easily. Hell, no! Not after she, in the course of the conversation, had learned he was a single man. "There might be another solution," she said. Thomas asked her what that was. "We could employ you – you know, pay your insurance and all of that." Mrs. Smart paused for a moment. "There is no way we could have security without insurance." I was growling all the while, and it was not pretence. My dislike for Mrs. Smart, who, by now, in her office, had procured a pot of tea for herself and Thomas. "I can offer you a decent wage." Thomas enquired what hours she had in mind for us to work.

"Sixty," she said, "five twelve-hour shifts. I can employ another man for the weekends."

"There's no need for that. Me and Martin can do weekends as well."

"Isn't that a bit much?"

"Not really. We've nothing much else to do."

"No?" Mrs. Smart feigned amazement, but I could sense that she was delighted. "I would have thought you had a lady friend."

"No, no such luck."

Mrs. Smart then took a more professional line, if only for a bit of show, and enquired about his employment history, and Thomas told her that he was a writer. "But not a very successful one."

"Have you been published?"

"I have. Short stories. They have been published here and there, in magazines and, a few years back, I had a lot of them in the Glasgow Herald. In The Saturday Extra section, but they don't use fiction anymore." Thomas paused. "It's why I want this job, that it would afford me time to write." Mrs. Smart declared she had known there was something different about him from the moment he had stepped inside her office. "I like to think I can judge people."

What twat, utter rubbish. This ancient huntress all coy and sweet and sipping delicately at her tea. "I smoke," she said. "Do you mind?" "Not at all, I could do with one myself." I could tell he was enjoying this, this flirt – and flirt it was, no mistake – with Mrs. Smart, who produced a cigarette from a box on her desk. "What happened to your last security?" he enquired

"One died, the other is retiring next week. They were with us for years, but times change and now we have *you*."

"Then I have the job?"

"If we can agree about wages. We haven't discussed the wages yet."

No, they hadn't; but, in event, they were to prove no problem, and so at last we had found a job.

***

"What do you make of her, that Mrs. Smart, Martin?"

A fucking cow.

"She's a bit of all right, don't you think?"

No, I don't; I think she's an old hag.

"I thought she was dead glamorous."

She's an ancient bitch.

"Nice legs, too."

I think you need an eye test.

"The backs of her hands were a bit wrinkled."

So was her face, and more than a bit.

"Still and all she's an attractive girl."

Girl! She must be sixty if a day.

"I think she fancies me."

She's desperate and looking for a last fling, that's all; before she becomes just too decrepit.

"*We'll* just need to wait and see what happens." But I knew what would happen. Thomas and Mrs. Smart. He was up for it and so was she, and not a thing that I could do about it. "I have high hopes, Martin."

I think you should see a psychiatrist.

"I wonder what her first name is?"

Skank!

"It was good luck finding her."

Good luck, my arse – she's as old as mammy.

"At least we've got a job if nothing else."

At home with Thomas, in our room. This *conversation*. Mrs. Smart. He was really taken on with her and I *really* thought he'd lost what sense he had. At least, for all I disagreed with it, their romance, Fidelma had been young, or, certainly, she was not old, unlike the wizened Mrs. Smart. What a frightful thing she must be, in the mornings without her war paint and her false teeth out and her face clapped-in. Thomas thought she was *a wee doll*. Some hope. Or he was fucking desperate, and that made for both of them. I'm using swear words here, because it was all swear words back them with him. Fucking this and fucking that and fucking cunt and I could go on. And on. The way it was. That fucking Mrs. Smart. She had set my big mate up, and that's a fact, if, and it grieves me to say it, he was a more than willing victim.

***

The factory was full of machinery and built some sort of aircraft engines. Not that we cared, what it built. Thomas had his haversack filled with food and drink for both of us. For a twelve-hour night we would surely need it. Food and drink. Our work as guards. Not, from what I could see, that there was much work to do. The place was surrounded by brick walls and steel gates and, big as it was – I would think about the size of two hockey pitches – it would have taken a lot of work, not to mention noise, to afford an illegal entry. Still. For all of that, I took to the guard work with a will. It was the way of my breed, the Doberman; or even part Doberman, as in my case. I was all ears the whole night long and in fact was a disappointment that we had no intruders. Thomas sat on an easy chair in a small office and appeared to read much more than write. Book after book, night after night. There was another chair I could curl up on or, alternatively, if I was feeling energetic, just go for a run around the place. The steel gates. I would listen at them for outside noises, but there was never anything. Not a whisper. The factory was down a lane, and well away from houses. It was a good hour's walk to get there and another hour back, so we were both well exercised. When he was not reading Thomas would speak to me, giving voice to his random thoughts. "I wish we were home, in bed, Martin."

I couldn't have agreed more. The lurking Mrs. Smart. It was her factory, and I was not liable to forget it. She was taking her time to make a move, but; for she was a wily one, and that for sure, the chances were she was biding her time not to appear too *easy*. She knew where he was, and could well afford to keep him waiting, hanging on. A couple of weeks. When it came to three, Thomas was giving up on it, her. "I'm beginning to think that she's forgotten all about me, Martin."

I wish she had, but knew she hadn't; my dog sense, that she was only holding out.

"Maybe she thinks she's too old for me"

I do too, but that won't stop her trying.

"I thought she was dead sexy."

And she knows it, that's why you got the job, you chump.

"But I might have been wrong, and she doesn't fancy me at all."

Give her time and you'll find out.

Thomas must have read a good section of the library by then. Our work as guards, if, as said, there was precious little guarding to be done. We could have been home in bed and nobody much the wiser, other than that Thomas had to hit a time clock at certain times throughout the night. A precaution that we were still there, on the job. Otherwise, we could have gone home and returned again to check out in the morning. Then, right out of the blue – in the early hours of the morning -What Mrs. Smart phoned. "Just to know how you are getting on." Thomas, I could see his surprise – he had thought she had forgotten him – assured her all was well and he was delighted she had thought to phone.

"I would have sooner, but I was away on business."

Fucking liar. You've been stringing him along, more like.

"But I will phone more often now."

"Please, do."

"I *will*."

And so do I, know you will, you conniving bitch.

"It was really nice of you to phone," Thomas said. "It can get pretty lonely here at night."

"I'm sure it can, but at least you've got Martin."

"I know I have." I was sitting looking up at him, and if only he could have read my head. *Hang up on her, or you'll be sorry.*

"How's the writing going?"

"Slow." *You can say that again, you've not written a fucking word.* "But I think I'm getting there."

"I'm sure you are." Mrs. Smart went on to say that she would love to read some of Thomas's short stories, the published ones. "You could leave them in the office for me." Thomas said he would do just that, which, of course, would be something to discuss when she phoned again. This seduction, could you call it that, the wily Mrs. Smart. She wished not to appear too pushy, cheap; as throwing herself at him, who was only too willing to catch her. "A wee doll."

"That was a pleasant surprise," he said, when they were disconnected. "I think she's taken a shine for me." I feigned a yawn. A show of disinterest. The rapturous Thomas. "I hope she likes the stories, Martin." I didn't, hope she liked them; but I knew she would,

75

or pretend she did. It was all, the whole shebang, a game to her. She had found a fucking oddball who, it must be said, had an upright look and a manly way and she did not know that he spoke to me and he was not for telling her. Fuck, no! He was not that daft. And he was no St Francis either, who, so it was said, thought nothing of speaking to animals. But that was all they had in common. St Francis had died when he was thirty-six and Thomas was now forty-one. It should, all things considered, have been the other way round. The gentle Francis who, out of love for his fellow man, had bequeathed his coat to a lowly beggar. Such a humble, most saintly saint. He could speak to creatures big and small and would have shunned away from Mrs. Smart. But Thomas was not the stuff of Francis who, by sheer example, had inspired the young St Anthony, he of the novena nights in St Francis's chapel in the Gorbals. Ironically, St Anthony – he was said to have held the baby Jesus – had died a young man too, well under forty. In later life, after me, a much different Thomas would visit both saints' shrines in Italy and, let's say, there was someone looking out for him.

***

After her first contact Mrs. Smart was seldom off the phone to Thomas, and, needless to say, she declared he was the best short story writer that she had ever read. "It's so alive, your writing."

"You flatter me."

"I do not; I mean every word that I say."

Some of her calls were at two; three o'clock in the morning, and it was soon revealed she was a widow and, "A little bit on the lonely side." After a week or so of this small talk Thomas asked her out. A date in a pub on a Saturday afternoon. Mrs. Smart was delighted to accept his invitation and added it would be her first date in six years, since Mr. Smart had passed away. Whether this was true or not is neither here nor there, but the way she said it implied that Thomas was a very privileged person. "I'll play it by instinct," Thomas said. "I don't want to fuck it up." There was little chance of that, the more than willing Lilian – they had gone on to first name's now - who, too, did not want to fuck it up but wanted fucked by a very privileged person.

Much as this is my own story, it has all to do with Thomas who *is* my story as I am his, and it will remain that way - in his head, me as a dog – until, what a surprise for him, when we meet again. It was a long time coming, Saturday; for Thomas, anyhow. "It's my first real date for years," he said, and I could not but wish, for him at least, that he had a better one than her. The made-up, too old Lilian. "I've been too busy with you, Martin." He had, it's true, and it occurred to me that it might have left him a sucker to painted face, however haggard.

"I'll not be drinking when I am with her." I thought he might need a drink when he was with her, but it was still good to know that, as far as the drinking was concerned, he might be wising up at last.

***

Thomas was in excellent form when we were again in the

factory on the Saturday night, after his day with Lilian. "I hope you didn't miss me too much, Martin." I had sulked a bit when he had come home, but I couldn't keep it up. That and I was curious about what had happened with him and Lilian. "We had a pub lunch and then she asked if I wanted to go home with her." *And I bet you did, you fucking rotter.* "I must say that she looked a treat, and she paid for everything." *A pub lunch!*

"She has a fantastic house, you want to see the grandeur."

No, I don't.

"Her bedroom must be the size of our whole house."

Is that a fact.

"I didn't think she'd be as easy."

I did.

"I was the first man she has had in six whole years, since her husband died."

But not for the want of trying, I don't think.

"I think she is a vulnerable woman, Martin."

Is she fuck, you fucking dough ball.

At that the telephone rang and, of course, it was her. "How are you, dear?"

"Missing you," Thomas said. "But I had a wonderful day, so I can't complain." Lilian said it was the same with her and she was missing him more than tongue could tell. "Next Saturday is so long to wait to see you again, my love." Thomas agreed that indeed it was, but they at least had something to look forward to. After more of similar twat — my ears pricked up in disbelief when I heard him call her baby — they ended the conversation with such words of endearment that they almost turned my stomach.

"She's missing me already, Martin."

I don't doubt that, because she'll be hard pressed to find a clown like you again.

"We had a really great day together, and the sex was fantastic."

Then you must be fucking easily pleased.

"She'd shame a woman half her age."

I think I'll just give up.

***

Mrs. Smart, Lilian, phoned a couple more times before they were to meet again. The same place at the same time, if she confessed to worry about his health. "You are working almost round the clock, my treasure." Thomas assured her he was fine, and she was not to trouble her pretty head worrying about him. "But I can't help it," Lilian said, and that she felt a bit like a slave driver, all the hours Thomas worked. "We'll need to do something about it." I was sure she would, one afternoon a week with Thomas was not enough for her. Or him, come to that; but we were paid by the hour, the bits of paper, and I knew he was loath to make do with less of them. "We'll think about it," he told her, "And try to work something out." Lilian was quick to jump right in. "It wouldn't affect your wages, I'd see to that – we could easily employ a weekend man."

***

"She's worried about me, Martin – the hours I am working."

No, she's not. Not a bit. The bitch only wants you to do less hours for her own ends, that you can spend more time with her. You must be cracked if you can't see that.

"It's not every day you meet a woman like her."

You can say that again, and I wish you hadn't.

But Thomas was flattered that Lilian was thinking about his welfare. So, she said, and I think he half believed her. A little flattery can go a long, long way and especially when, as in this case, the recipient was none too used to it. Not of late, anyhow. The drunken bruiser he had been. So, in a way, this dramatic change, that he was in demand and a treasure to boot, it had to raise his ego. Lilian had seen to that, her suggestion that he worked lesser hours but did not lose a single piece of paper. *I'm surprised she didn't offer you a pay rise, for working lesser hours.* "I have to say," Thomas said, "that it didn't take too long for me to get her knickers down."

You didn't think it would, did you?

"She's got nice smooth legs and a good arse, I'll say that for her."

80

And plenty of bits of paper, if you play your cards right.

"She wears a gold chain round her ankle."

Isn't that nice.

"She's the first woman I've had who wears a chain round her ankle."

Then you've been slow, because I've seen plenty of human bitches with gold chains round their ankles.

"It made her look like an Arabian girl."

Girl!

"The only thing, I think she could be bossy."

Think!

"She's certainly assertive." Thomas lit a cigarette. "It's what worries me about her."

This was the first sensible thing I had heard him say with regard to Lilian, that he was worried enough to be apprehensive. This after *one* date. A bossy boots with a gold chain round her ankle! She would not boss him, and that for sure. He was of the rebel kind and would remain that way until he died. The way to him as I well knew, and had known from the very first, was by affection. Should Lilian come on too heavy he would not be slow in telling her to take a hike, to fuck off. It was that simple. Thomas. He would meet aggression with aggression, without a thought to the consequences. His was a hard, unbreakable pride and, even if he had wanted to, he could not buckle under. Not for wealth or Helen of Troy, never mind for an old bag like Lilian. So, the chances were, clashing personalities, for a short affair as, I think, most of his romances were, had been. No wonder. Apart from his pride, which was bad enough, Thomas was a very mixed-up man. It couldn't be helped and I loved him dearly, and I still love him. Some hairy moments, like the Lilian business; that he was dropping me to be with her, but they would pass over. Come and go, while I remained. Loyal and true and missing him incredibly when he ditched me for a woman"

I had come to adjust to his one-night stands – and there were more of them than I have mentioned here – but Lilian was different. A true threat. She was after more than a one-night stand, and if I was jealous of her, she was jealous of me. The hold I had on Thomas. I was much more than a dog to him, as I am sure you will know by now. "I sometimes wonder how I came by you," he would tell me often. "I'm beginning to think you were always there." How true, and the pity was that he did not know it, that I *had* been always there. Not that I did either, not then; not that I could put my paw upon, if, all the time, I was aware that we were altogether different from the usual dog and master. Thomas must have sensed this too and had to know how he felt for me was, well, to say the least, unusual.

It was more than he could ever feel for Lilian, or any of his other floozies, and he knew that and so did I, and so did Mammy and Mary.

An aside to this, another problem – for Thomas, that is, he

could not bed a woman in view of me. No, and forgetting jealousy, I might have thought that they were fighting and have bitten her, and badly. I was by now, his so-called pet, a good eighty pounds of bone and muscle and long sharp teeth and was as quick as a flash and felt fit to fight a timber wolf. Or two of them if it came to that. Thomas would have had little chance with me in a fight, a real one. Not that it would come to that, but he had to protect his bitches. He had to protect *me*. So, there was always a door at the very least to lock me out before the humphing, moans and groans and the occasional scream, began.

***

Once again, come Saturday; Thomas bathed and shaved – not that he was an unclean man, but he did not shave just every day – and donned new, fresh, clothes for his date with Lilian. Neither Mammy or Mary knew where he was going but, left alone with me, for I could not help but start to howl, they hoped he would not be gone too long. Nor *could* he be, for he had to be home about seven o'clock to for us to be at our work on time. But even that, eight hours at best, is a long time to spend with a howling dog. Still and all they had to know he was due a little freedom, away from me who did not want to be away from him. Not for a moment, much less for the whole of a fucking day. But there was not a thing that I could do, except, perhaps, before he went, to sulk in disapproval. I could contain myself, the missing Thomas, for an hour or so, but then, to the dread of our pack, I would begin to howl. As a wolf. In the wild, in some frozen forest. It was something deep, rooted in me; a forlorn call as old as time, from the depths of my being, that, to put it mildly, I was lonely. My horny, gallivanting pal. He never saw this side of me, for it only showed when he was not there. Which was as well for him, but a torture for Mammy and Mary. And our neighbours, the whole district. No-one complained, for it happened rarely, a full day's howling, but I am sure that they all were glad when Thomas returned.

"She's looking for a weekend man, so I could spend more time with her." Thomas sat in his chair with me at his feet, my ears pricked up. "But I told her that I can't leave you."

"Good old Thomas, that you can't leave me."

'She thought I was crazy, but I don't care – and it would have been no good anyhow, all night with her, because I'd have only been worried about how you were."

Thank fuck for that.

"I told her that the afternoons were a better time for me."

But not for her, because she wants you nights."

"There was no further mention of a weekend man, but that's the way the cookie crumbles."

You're telling me.

'Lilian was dead upset, that I couldn't spend all night with her." Thomas lit a cigarette. "We might be out of a job soon, for all I know." *We got by before she came and we'll get by again when she is gone.*

"She's a good wee fuck, though." Thomas looked reflective. "I knew she would be, but she's even better than I thought." *At her age?* "There must be some truth in the saying, the older the fiddle the better the tune. Anyway, she's agreed to take a half day off and meet me Wednesday afternoons." Thomas looked at his watch and then rose from his chair. "I am fed up punching the time clocks, Martin." I was up on my paws, and trotting in front. A walk around the factory. I wished that Thomas would walk more often, but he preferred to sit and read. He was supposed to be writing, but suffering a block. "I can't get two words to three, and it would be a waste of time to even try."

I hardly cared what he did, not, that is, when he was with me. Read or write, it was all the same; if, at times, I could sense he was frustrated that he was stuck, his writing.

Lilian was stuck with him, for the present at least. She had agreed to take a half day off that they could meet mid-week. I had the impression, for all she was, "a good wee fuck," that Thomas was not so stuck on her. Not now, after she had thought him crazy that he would not leave me for a night. That and he was clocking on that she was far vulnerable. More a hard-headed business woman who suited herself by going with him because he was the best that she could get. At her age, and it had to be a cross to her that she was old and had to make do with a man like him who, for all he was presentable, had no social graces.

"She said she was in love with me." We were back in the

office, a musing Thomas. His thing with Lilian. "But I bet she's said the same to plenty of men in her time." At that, right then; as once before, the telephone rang and we both knew it was *her*. "Are you alright my darling?"

"Why shouldn't I be?"

"I didn't mean to be cross with you, I hope you know that."

"I do."

He did?

"It was more that I was astonished that you couldn't leave Martin for even one night. You must admit that it did sound strange, and it's not like Martin is a poodle." Lilian let out with a short, false laugh. "I think you've been alone for too long, Thomas."

"I'm not alone."

"Do you mean that you have Martin?"

"What else?"

"What about before you had him?"

"I thought I would become a monk."

"No, you didn't." This time Lilian's laugh was real. "You're a strange one, aren't you?"

"If you think that."

"What else can I think, and I wonder what manner of strange man I've fallen in love with."

That pleased Thomas. I could tell. He had been quite offhand with her up till then. Now he had the lip to say he loved her too, and more —that he would die if she chucked him.

I could only look on and marvel at this tripe. A man in love. So, he said. No further thoughts to a monastery. "We were born to be together, sweetheart."

What a load of crap, you fucking liar. You'll never get to heaven, the way you're going.

"I mean that, Lilian."

Lilian said she knew he did. "And I absolutely agree with you, for I've never been in love like this before." She waffled on romantically, and, "I thought true love had passed me by."

And so, it has, you stupid bitch.

Thomas assured her that it hadn't, and, "I thought the very same until I met you."

"You did?"

"I did."

"I'll make you so happy," Lilian promised.

"You already have."

"Then happier."

"That would be impossible."

This guff, really sickening stuff – I wished I had put my paws over my ears – went on and on. A good ten minutes. Undying love and all of that and I have to say I was truly glad when, at last, Thomas hung up the phone. "She said again that she loves me, Martin."

But you don't believe her, do you?

"It's hard to know just what to think, how *she* thinks."

That you are fucking nuts, that's how she thinks – it's the only thinking she can think.

"I have to say that I might have judged her harshly."

You don't think that, not really; surely.

"She seemed a changed woman."

In a few hours?

"She was a fucking nasty piece today, I can tell you – after I explained that I couldn't spend the night with her."

I can well imagine.

'She's a woman of spirit."

More a woman of spite.

Thomas said it was good she had phoned. "It goes to show that she cares about me."

It was a bag of fucking lies she spun and you spun her.

"You have no idea the trouble I've had with women, Martin."

That's what you think.

"Fucking disasters, the lot of them."

Why was that, Thomas?

"Most guys of my age have been married for years and some of them even have fucking grandchildren."

But you chose to live wild and free and not giving a damn for anybody, least of all a fucking wife.

"I sometimes wish I had children."

You might have some you don't know about.

"As it is I don't even have a home of my own. Lilian thought it was odd, that I still stay with my mother

That's only because no other woman would put up with you, for you have lived with a few, haven't you?"

"One sure thing, I'll never live with Lilian."

I hope not. He didn't. Nor did he spend a single night with her. The romance lingered on in the day-time only. We continued to work seven, twelve hour shifts weekly in the factory. There were nights when Thomas was exhausted and he would sit in his chair and sleep. This went on all through the autumn – we had begun to work for Lilian in August – and into winter. November and December. Another Christmas and New Year. We worked all through it. No, that year, Midnight mass for him with Mammy. Thomas spent Christmas day with Lilian who drove him home and then drove *us* to the factory. It was not, not for me, a very good Christmas. Lilian had cooked a Christmas dinner for both of them. A homely affair, I'm sure. Roast turkey and candles, a bottle of wine. So, Thomas told me, when we were alone that night. "Lilian became a little tipsy, but I didn't touch a single drop." For the very first time I wished he had, and more than a drop. The whole of the fucking bottle. Lilian would have seen a different side to her lover then. The police might even have become involved. As it was, they had a peaceful time. I have no idea what he bought her, but she bought him a big gold watch "What do you make of it, Martin?" He asked, showing me his wrist.

I think it will be good for you to pawn the next time you are skint.

"It's solid gold."

Then you'll get more paper for it.

"Lilian was a splendid hostess."

I wish she'd go away.

"She was hinting about a holiday in Tenerife where it is warm at this time of year."

I don't like the sound of this.

"She's fed up with the winter here."

This sounds like trouble to me.

"Anyhow, I told her that I couldn't go — that I had you to consider and I think that she understands."

I don't.

Thomas looked at his new watch. "It's a super gift she

bought me."

I could only offer him a lick, which could hardly compare to a chunk of gold.

"I felt like a fucking gigolo." Thomas frowned. "You see, Martin, she's older than I thought she was."

Tell me more.

"She's sixty-four. You wouldn't believe it. I still can't, but I saw her old age pension book lying on a table and she saw that I had seen it and was all embarrassed and I felt rotten. I really did. I mean, who would have thought she was a pensioner?" *Me. But I can't speak, so I couldn't say.* "I had the book in my hand and she was looking at me and I looked at her and then she said she but hoped it did not matter." Thomas looked at his watch again. "Of course, I told her that it didn't. We were just after making love, and she had given me my gift and I think I was more embarrassed than she was." Thomas paused, clearly perplexed. "I thought she was fifty, fifty-five at most; but nothing like sixty-four. But I don't suppose it matters any, if I wish I had never seen that pension book. Dead on cue, as it were, the telephone rang and we both knew who it was on the other end. "Thomas, darling."

"Lilian."

"Are you okay, sweetie?"

"Why shouldn't I be?"

"Oh, you know – well, you were surprised, weren't you?"

"I've forgotten all about it."

"I haven't. I know that you thought that I was much younger. What happened to me is a woman's nightmare."

"Don't let it be, because what has age to do with love?"

"Many people think a lot. Most men go for younger women."

"I'm not most men."

"I know that, Thomas – but it was a bit of a shock for you, I would think."

"It was. I thought you were in your forties."

Liar!

"I feel like I'm in my twenties when I am with you –did you know that, Thomas?

"No, I didn't, but it makes me happy that you do."

Lilian changed the subject. "I really wish we could go on holiday to Tenerife. It would be a dream come true to have you all to myself for two whole weeks. Promise me you'll think about it, Thomas."

"I will."

"A couple of weeks away from Martin won't kill him, and it would do you the world of good."

Thomas declared he was not so sure of that. "I'd worry about him, as I've already told you." Lilian said she knew that he had, "but

you've a life the same as him, and he might even like it in a kennel."
*No, I wouldn't, and anyhow – for I know Thomas much better than you do – I
won't be going into any fucking kennel.*

"I couldn't do it, Lilian, put Martin in a kennel."

"I thought you said that you would think about it."

"I've thought about it."

"This is crazy."

"Crazy or not, it's the way I feel."

"You're letting a dog rule your life, and putting him in front
of me."

"I can't help that."

***

"She's not too pleased, I don't think," Thomas said when he
put down the phone, "but there's nothing I can do about it." *No, not
a thing – why do you think I chose you?* "I told her before –before I knew
her age, that is – how it is with me and you, and I think she thinks
I'm crazy."

You are, a little; but we'll try and keep it quiet.

"I can see us without a job before too long, because she
thinks I'm putting you in front of her."

Thinks.

"I've saved a few bobs, so it won't be the end of the world if we get sacked."

No, it won't, and you'll soon find another bitch for me to loathe.

"But I did like her."

She's not chucked you yet.

"It's a pity this had to happen, that she wanted me to go on holiday with her." Thomas sat smoking. A mug of coffee. "I mean, I don't care how old she is." *That's obvious* "We'll see what happens when we meet next week." *I hope she chucks you.* "I might talk her round, who knows?" Thomas, for such a man as him, was strangely upset about his rift with Lilian. His new gold watch? It was a whopper, but more, and worse, I knew he was fond of her who was fond of him, if only because he was her last chance, let's get that one straight. A younger Lilian would not have looked at Thomas who, for all he was well read and courteous, was penniless and had few social graces. She would have viewed him as awkward lout, and who could blame her? Not Thomas. He had been around and knew the score, his own shortcomings. The problem was, as I saw it, that Lilian could not see hers, that, in truth, she was lucky to have him but still felt fit to threaten. *A good boot in the arse is what she needs.* Thomas said he did not want to lose her, or lose our job, but then again he would not be bullied.

***

A couple of weeks later Lilian went on holiday to Tenerife, alone. This was good news for me, *and* Thomas. He was becoming to be a bit fed up with her by now, her moaning; that he preferred a dog to her. It was the ultimate insult how she saw things. Thomas said he could not care less, and he had no choice anyhow. "You can look after yourself, but Martin can't."

"You think more of him than you do of me."

"Whatever you think."

"What else can I think?"

"You could try to understand me better."

"I don't want to understand a man who prefers a dog to me."

So, a stormy time, after Christmas time and New Year; and the wonder was that we were still in a job when Lilian left for Tenerife, if, as Thomas said, it was only because she did not have time to sack us. "I'm in her bad books, you know that, Martin?" *I do.* The next two weeks were like old times, just me and Thomas. I would doubt he gave a thought to Lilian, who, however, was still there, lurking in the background. Her revenge, but we were hardly quaking. I had never seen Thomas quake for anything, and he would certainly not quake for her. How things can change. This fall-out. It had been sudden as a thunder clap, and Thomas complained that Lilian was, "A wicked thing, completely without compassion." God alone knows what she said about him, and I think they both knew that their affair was over. *Finito.* Lilian had bought him his big gold watch a week too soon. Thomas laughed, looking at it. "She'll be hopping mad; I can tell you that, Martin."

The silly bitch, it serves her right.

"She'll be home soon."

You don't need to tell me that.

There were no phone calls when she did come home. Rather an icy sort of silence. Thomas said that maybe she thought he should be phoning her. As for me, I was still enjoying my tins of Chappie, and would go on enjoying them for a few weeks longer. In the factory, our work as guards. Thomas was beginning to think that Lilian might not be as bad as he had thought. "We're still in a job, after all." But he spoke too soon, and a couple of days later a letter arrived at our home address informing Thomas that our services were now terminated.

"Just like that," Thomas said, tossing the letter aside, "that fucking screwball, Lilian."

An aside to this, the company - Lilian was the chair person - had to pay a month' wages in lieu of notice.

"It's nothing to them, and I am sure she thought it was worth it to try and punish me."

She's a woman scorned and you should be glad that there is nothing more she can do to punish you.

"It was good while it lasted, money for nothing or very little," Thomas said, "but it had to end, one way or another."

***

Out of our job we began a new novena, the nine consecutive Tuesdays. This would take us into spring, April or early May. You could, week after week, see the difference in the nights, how they lengthened out. By the end of our novena there was an extra two or even three hours of brightness. "St Anthony's, Martin." Thomas said, but he did not need to tell me. It was easy to know a Tuesday night, because he was much cleaner, washed and shaved, and Mary came with us, and that was fine with me. It was because of Mary that we were at the novena, where she was going anyhow, and, in a way, we just sort of tagged along. Mary was more into religion than Thomas and she attended mass on Sundays and saints' days, while he didn't. No. I would doubt that Thomas had been to Sunday mass since he was a boy. But he liked the novena and I *loved it*. The walk down there and back again and no Lilian. Mrs. Smart. She had taken the humph, and, if I could, I would have said a prayer in thanksgiving for that.

***

For a bit of a change, we now went to a different field at night. This place was on top of a hill and you could see the lights of the city spread out below. There were the usual dogs and dog walkers and we soon made new friends, of a sort. Two men, Adam and Mark, who owned a King Charles Spaniel. This was a really tiny dog and, at first, when I came near, either Adam or Mark would snatch it up to cradle in their arms. The small dog's name was Gigi, and she was given to running away, back to her house as fast as her little legs could carry her, if, that was, her masters were not looking. Adam and Mark put up with this because they were both fond of Gigi, and more than fond of each other too. Indeed. They had been together for more than two years and were still very much in love. Adam was young and affected, but Mark was older and very masculine. A short, stocky bull- like man who had a big black beard and a pugnacious look and it was my good luck that we had found two such. We had completed by now another full novena and there had been women of course. Thomas out on a few dates, for, when he came home, I could smell the bitches from him. But one-night stands and nothing like the possessive, clinging, Lilian. Or Fidelma, come to that. Thank fuck again that she had moved, gone away. At least Adam and Mark were no threat to me, if, I have to say, that Gigi was a poor companion. "She sleeps in our bed," Adam declared, "but I am afraid Mark does not like it." Mark said he surely didn't. "I think it unhygienic." Thomas said on holiday that we slept together. "I didn't give it a single thought." Adam said that neither did he. "I think that Mark is an old fuddy- duddy."

"Less of the old." Mark's beard appeared to bristle. "God knows, and I am fond of her but I still think that she should sleep in her own basket rather than in bed with us." And so it went, the happy if sometimes bickering couple; who, we were to learn - shades of Thomas in his affair with Lilian – had forfeited a holiday in San Francisco because Adam would not leave Gigi. "But he's forgiven me, haven't you, *sweetie?" Adam was something of a tease, teasing Mark, who was the older, about* Thomas's age, in his early forties. "I felt like slinging Gigi out of the window at the time," he said. "I mean, a holiday in San Francisco." "I wouldn't have spoken to you ever again had you done that" *Mark said it was only a thought.* But you must admit I had good reason to be angry." In answer to that Adam, who was cuddling Gigi, reached across and kissed Mark full on the lips. "Love you loads."

Mark was pleased, you could tell. Why not? He had forfeited a trip to San Francisco for such kisses. "Love you, too," he said.

Thomas said there had to be come and go, and the main thing was that they were still together.

"Forever," Adam said.

"Ditto," said Mark.

Adam asked Thomas how long he had been married?

"I'm not married."

"But you have been married?"

"No."

"That's surprising."

"Do you think"

"I certainly do, a man of your age. You're not gay by any chance?"

"No, but I have sometimes wished I was."

For myself, this talk of sexuality, I am proud to say that it had been some time since I last embarrassed Thomas. Perhaps St Anthony had something to do with this, that I had become well behaved in that direction.

***

One of the days, in the early evening, we happened to meet Mark on the street and, he was in rough working togs, discovered he was a bricklayer. "Surprised?" he asked. "Not at all." "There's a few like me in the building game." Mark was in a high, good humour. "We're going out tonight, myself and Adam to celebrate my birthday." Thomas said that was good. "You've got to let your hair down sometimes." "If I had much hair." Mark touched his head. "I'm a half bald old coot."

"You have a fine beard."

"Mark thinks I should buy a wig."

"I think you are okay just the way you are."

"That's kind of you to say so."

"And you're not an old coot."

"I'm forty."

Thomas said that he did not look it, and, "Forty is far from old."

"It's more than double Adam's age."

"I don't see why that should matter."

"It doesn't, not for me – but I sometimes worry that it might to Adam."

"I would doubt to that, because he's nuts about you."

"I hope he is. Believe me. It's a long time since I felt about a guy the way I feel for Adam."

"I think the feeling's mutual."

Mark asked Thomas if he would join him in a near-by pub. "For a couple of beers and a wee dram."

"I wish I could, but I'm a strict teetotaler, Mark."

What a bare-faced lie but it did the trick and got rid of Mark who, to me, both him and his boyfriend and their little dog Gigi, were a pain in the arse. A swipe of my paw would have done for Gigi, so I much preferred, when we were in the field, to meet with a woman named Maggie and her dog, a giant schnauzer named Toby. He was up for fun, Toby was, and we would rough and tumble, and, even better, Maggie was a buck-toothed, humpbacked hag who was enough to put even Thomas off, and that is saying something. For all of this, her ill-looks, Maggie was married and had been married for years to a taxi driver by the name of Willie. He was retired now, Willie was, and so too was Maggie. This, for me, was another good thing about our new friend, that she was old, in her seventies. But she was all there in the top deck and Thomas liked her and I was pleased he liked her for I liked to play with Toby. He was big and thick and a match for me in our rough and tumble. It was all good fun, the schnauzer and me, if, perhaps, the occasional growl when things got out of hand. But not too much and neither of us was ever injured. Toby had courage, I'll say that for him, but I was quicker and just as strong and in a real fight I would have done for him, no problem. Thomas was aware of that, and more than aware that I could sometimes lose the place and so kept a close eye on our mauling. "Trust me to get a dog like you," he would say. "You've got to let up a little, Martin." I'm only competitive. And so I was, my play with Toby. Far better I was on top of him than he was on top of me. But the problem was, this roughhousing, that Maggie became alarmed that it could spark off into a real fight with Toby getting the worse of it. It would not have happened, not a real fight, but she was not for taking chances and so began avoiding us.

At this time there were stories about a fierce dog that roamed the field and often savaged other dogs. I was lucky and did not meet it, but the same could not be said for Toby, who, strong as he was and full of heart, was mauled and badly bitten. It had to cost a lot of the wherewithal for him to be half-way well again. As for the dog that did the damage nothing more was heard about him – or his master, come to that – and he was not seen again. But he had wrecked poor Toby who, on the few times that we met again, was anything but boisterous. A timid shadow of his former self and Thomas, seeing this, admonished me to change my ways. "I don't want to see you mangled, Martin." Well, neither did I. What dog would? But there are times when a dog must fight. That or lose all face and run away, and it was not in my nature to run away. But that in the future, when I would fight for my life, and I paid little heed to

Thomas. He was always on about this or that and Adam and Mark and," Mark is older than he says. I would think he's fifty if a day. I don't know who he thinks he's kidding."

Not you, anyhow.

"He's really just a sugar daddy."

What the fuck's a sugar daddy?

"It's a while since we've seen them, Adam and Mark – I wonder how they're doing?"

***

A few nights later we met Adam in the field and Thomas told him: "I could fall for you myself." Adam smiled. Even white teeth in his lipsticked mouth. "I thought perhaps you – well, you know, might have thought me distasteful."

"You must be joking."

"No, I'm not; because some men do."

"Not me."

"Then I take it you like the way I am?"

"I do. You look gorgeous."

"It's sweet of you to say so, Thomas."

I was a bit bemused by all of this. The glamorous Adam. He wore a short blond wig and a shorter skirt and had a fake beauty spot on his left cheek. It, for whatever reason, the beauty spot, appeared alluring. He was in a short tight skirt and long white legs and was wearing high heeled shoes. Yet for all of that; and he was a beautiful girl, there was a queer hard edge, that he was not a one to trifle with. When Thomas asked him where Mark was, he was informed that he was at home nursing a sore head. "We had a row and I cracked him over his silly head with a wine bottle." Adam giggled in a girlish way. "It was an empty one."

"It must have been a bit of a row if you did that."

"He accused me of cheating and I saw red,"

"And Mark saw stars."

Adam giggled again. "I suppose he did, but I was hot and bothered and very, very agitated."

Thomas said he felt sure that it was just a lover's tiff. "And I bet you feel the same, don't you?"

"I do not. He's dead jealous and thinks he owns me, if you want to know the truth."

"He could be insecure, and I know he'd hate to lose you."

"Did he tell you he was forty?"

"He did."

"He's closer to sixty."

"I thought about fifty."

Adam pursed his lips and shook his head. "He's fifty-four."

"That's a bit away from sixty."

"It's a lot older than forty." Adam was in a bitchy mood, that for sure. "The party was ruined because he became suspicious about me and another guy."

"That shows how much he's in love with you."

"You mean obsessed."

"It's something the same."

Adam said he hoped not. "Obsession is unhealthy."

I was standing next to Thomas during this conversation, love and obsession and Mark at home nursing a broken head. It was all crazy, as I saw it; and I also thought, my dog's nose – for it whiffed a person who was not Mark - that Adam might have been unfaithful. We dogs, some of us, can pick up on things much quicker than most humans. Adam said that he had better get back to check up on the injured Mark. "I would not be in the least surprised if he's called in the cops and claimed that I assaulted him."

Thomas said he doubted that. "I told you that he's nuts about you."

"Enough to forget I smashed his head?"

"He'll forgive and forget, don't worry."

"But will I forgive him? Adam asked. "I was as good as accused of cheating."

***

"He's a boy with spirit, that Adam."

Or a conceited girl.

"Hot bloodied too, hitting Mark over the head with a bottle."

More vicious, I'd say.

"I tried to stick up for Mark, but I think that Adam's fed up with him."

Absolutely.

"But it's got nothing to do with us."

No, but it is the sort of thing that amuses you.

"Still, I would need to say that Adam is a beguiling boy."

A dangerous fucker, more like,

"I'm sure that he'll make up with Mark."

I'm not.

***

Thomas's amusement. The stranger it was the better for him. I had first noticed this odd trait the night I bit the policeman. It had been a howl for him – after we had got out of it, that was – and well worth his black eye. Then, later still, when he had heard that the bitten cop, who was far from popular with his mates, had been slipped a horse laxative, he could not contain his glee. Even the tramp, William – the guy he had bailed out of jail – had been a laugh, when he had been returned back to the Christmas crib. "St Joseph looked angry to see him back again." Mammy said surely not. "St Joseph is only a statue." "Then the statue looked angry, and I can't say that I blamed it. I mean, even a statue can do without the likes of him." Mammy said it was more like the priest who would have been annoyed to have William back. "He fouled the crib, I understand." "The dirty thing," Thomas said, but he could not hide his laughter. The crib and William was the best laugh he had had in years. "No wonder St Joseph was angry." Mammy said she sometimes wondered what had become of William. Thomas suggested that he might have reformed. "You know, had a spiritual awakening and all of that. If ever a man was in the right place at the right time to have a spiritual awakening it was him."

Mammy said she did not think it funny. "The poor man must have wondered what had happened, that he was back in the crib again."

"It was the best place for him." William and the stricken cop and the haughty dressed up Adam were the stuff that made him laugh, such was his sense of humour.

***

By this time, my time with Thomas, he had completed a novel. It was a weird work, what else? He had had it out to publishers who, and almost by return, had it back to him. This caused Thomas to believe that it had gone unread, and, this was before the computer age with books on line and all of that, he complained about the postage that it was costing him. The novel must have been to London and back again a good twenty times before, by chance; by way of a book by the Glasgow writer, James Kelman – who, Kelman, would go on to win the Booker prize – he thought to send it to an Edinburgh publisher named Polygon, who, surprisingly, and a delight to Thomas, accepted it. "It's only a small publisher," he explained to Mammy and Mary, "but you never know, it might be picked up by a major one." Mary said she hoped it was. "It's about time you made some money out of writing." Mammy agreed. "But I wouldn't put much hope on it," she warned. "There's an awful lot of books out there." Thomas said he was disappointed by the small advance. "One hundred and fifty pounds. I used to earn more than that in one week when I was a navvy.

Back in the past, before me, Thomas had worked with a pick and shovel on a hydroelectric site in the Scottish Highlands. Mary said he had drunk that money and she hoped that he would not drink the book advance. Thomas said he would give half of it to mammy and open a bank account with the other half. "It'll be a first for me, to have money in the bank. I should explain that we, or he, had been paid in cash, in brown pay packets, when we had worked for Mrs. Smart and I assumed that it had been the same when he was working as a navvy. When the cheque arrived from Polygon; Mary cashed it and, afterwards, they had gone to a local bank where, at last, for it should have been much sooner – he was in his forties, after all – Thomas opened a bank account. The book was scheduled for publication in some nine months' time when it was understood he would be paid a further one hundred and fifty pounds. "But at least I'll be a published author." This was no mean thing, not from his background, to have achieved; succeeded too, and he did not know, not then, that his book would come to nothing.

Indeed, for bad sales; something like forty copies sold, it would take a bit of beating. But that in the future and, when his book was first accepted, Thomas had been full of hope that he had written a best seller.

***

When we next met up with Adam and Mark, they were again the best of friends, if a shift in their relationship. A chastened Mark who seemed a little in awe of Adam, who, it was clear, was not the sort to be abused. No, sir. So, all in all he was pretty meek, but it was clear that he still loved Adam, who, this time around, was back again as a slender youth, if not a very manly one. "I believe Adam told you about our little tiff," Mark said.

"He did."

"It was all about nothing."

"I wouldn't say that," Adam's voice was surprisingly commanding and all at odds with how he looked. "You were in the wrong and hopefully you know it."

Mark confessed that he had offended Adam. "But I didn't really mean it."

Thomas said that you always hurt the one you love. "I don't

know why, but it's very true."

I hope that you don't mean hurting me.

Adam said he had been badly hurt. "I was shocked that Mark could think such things about me."

Mark said he had been out of order but that it was all in the heat of the moment. "I've been down on my knees to Adam ever since."

I don't doubt that

***

Early that summer we went on a caravan holiday to a sea-side town in the south of England, where, for the first in a long time, Thomas got drunk. The drinking began in Birmingham, where we had to change buses. There was a couple of hours between them and, after I had fed me in a park of sorts, he found a pub where he drank some beer and whisky and I could *feel* the change in him. A reckless, aggressive man. Had Adam or Mark met up with this Thomas they would not have hung around for long. A latent violence in his nature that, when he drank, was then exposed? Not that he was ever tough with me, I can't claim that; but, for there are many other violent men, I was frightened for him.

The next bus took us further south, to the caravan he had booked for our so-called holiday. Thomas now with a good drink in him, but he was still okay and with his wits about him. That was all to change when we arrived at the seaside town. This about nine at night and I could smell the sea and the town had a couple of pubs and an off-sales, where Thomas bought whisky and beer and enquired the way to our caravan. It was not too far, as things turned out. A cream-coloured van that was secluded in woods and, thankfully, the drunken Thomas, it was beside a spring of fresh water. Drink. If I had thought to know what booze can do, I was mistaken. This new Thomas who, it would be fair to say was next door to a werewolf. The difference was that his blood was whisky and, for a time at least, he could not get enough of it. Morning, night, and through the night. He did not shave or wash and the wonder was that he escaped the attention of the law, the local constabulary. There were a couple of near things, as, in the off-sales, where he pushed aside a portly man who, obviously, did not like to be pushed aside. "I protest at your behaviour, Sir." "Fuck off, fattie." Things like that and I should mention that I was off the lead and following him from the caravan to the off-sales and back again about two or three times a day. More whisky and beer but not a thought to dog food. It was as if he had forgotten me, of my existence. Still, as is the way of my kind, I had no option but to put up with it. At least the brook was there, so I was not thirsty; and, had this continued, I would have gone foraging. There were numerous small animals in the woods that I would have figured out a way to catch. A return to the wild, to my wolf ancestors. It would not have been hard, *two* savages; and you can accustom to almost anything in this world.

It did not come to that for the simple reason that Thomas ran out of the wherewithal. "This whole thing has been a fuck up,

Martin," he told me when, finally, he had recovered his wits. "I don't know how we will get out of this one." And neither did I. A wrecked caravan with all of its windows smashed due to his drunken stagger. "I've no money for the bus fare home." *Then you'll just need to get it, because we've got to get out of this place, and sharply*

Thomas by now, this about five days on from Birmingham; from his first drink in the pub, had a fair-sized scruffy-looking beard. It was something of a phenomenon, which I had noticed before, that when he drank his beard grew at an alarming rate. But never so much as then, in the caravan in the seaside town. I thought there might be beasties in it because half of the time he had slept outside, on the grass, and his beard was nice and warm, welcoming. What a nuisance that beard must have been, for Thomas was always scratching. But stuck with it because his were too shaky to attempt to cut it off. I say cut, with a pair of scissors, for no razor with have done the trick with such a beard.

"What will we do, Martin?"

You'll think of something.

And so, he would, for a man of resource if nothing else, and I trusted him to get us out, away from this place; the hateful caravan, and back to safety.

"You look a bit skinny, mate."

That's because you've starved me.

"This caravan's been fucking trashed."

It was you who did it.

"But if we're not here when it is discovered I can say it was not me."

Then we better get a move on.

Thomas's bag was still unopened, so we were ready for a swift getaway. But not right now, on the moment. Thomas had to wait till night, when, in the dark, he could burgle a shop for the fare to get us home. "I used to be good at it when I was young, burgling shops."

You're in a bit of a state to burgle a shop.

"We don't have any other option."

No, we didn't, but what an option. Thomas would go to jail if he got caught, and, if he was, it was the end of the line for me. I would attack the arresting officers, but cops have clubs and the chances were that they would smash my brains out. But as Thomas said and I agreed there was no other option.

In the night in the town, Thomas with a jemmy that – a short, straight, piece of iron that was crooked at one end - he had picked up someplace. I was still off of the lead, but I was used it by now, this following after him. Thomas tried the backdoor of a pub at first, but it was too locked-up. "Like fucking Fort Knox," he said to me, before he tried a dairy. The lock on the backdoor of this one gave easily, and "Come in, Martin".

Hurry it up, fuck's sake! Thomas behind the counter, rifling the till. A good few notes of the money to get us home, and, from a shelf, a couple of tins of dog food.

Good on you, Thomas

"Let's go, Martin."

I'm all for that

And so, we went. A brisk walk through the sleeping town with not a soul in sight. Back in the caravan Thomas fed me a tin of the dog food and tallied up the cash that he had stolen. "There's a lot more here than I think we need, Martin."

That's good, as long as you don't think to drink it

But I knew he wouldn't. The bout had passed and it would be months, or even a year before he thought to drink again.

In the lead-up to this escape he had discovered there was a bus that left from the seaside town for Birmingham in the early morning, this about two hours after he had robbed the dairy. So, we had little time to make our way to the stop and board it. Thomas with his unopened bag and a smaller one with my stuff, a bottle of water and my feeding bowls, which, needless to say – I had eaten my meal out of soup dish – had gone unopened.

I was back on the leash, what a delight; that I *belonged*, walking to the bus stop. A sober Thomas. He was still young, or, more precisely, far from old and, seemingly, none the worse for his drinking binge. A touch of the shakes and a bit of a smell, but there were few passengers on the bus and our journey was uneventful.

But once again, in Birmingham, there was a gap between buses, the bus that would take us back to Glasgow. This did not bother me at all, as, once again, I had a kind and caring master. In control. A Thomas who knew what he was about. It was a huge remove from the imbecile in the caravan in the seaside town that we had left behind us.

To help pass the time we went to the same park as we had been in before and, once again, I was fed and watered. Stolen food, but who was caring? We had chanced too much with our burglary to give a hoot about it now. Some things are better forgotten, and that was one, and, in truth, for such a chance, we were *due* the gains that we had made.

In the park, could you call it that; for a small grassy square with some shrubbery and wooden benches. I was off of the lead because there was nobody there but us. A peaceful day, place, until, that was a man and his dog came into the square and he sat down on a bench across from us. He was dressed in jeans and a string vest that emphasized his belly. He had his dog on the lead, what was just as well, for it was an aggressive sort of bull breed with a huge head and deep chest and very, very dangerous.

This on a glance for it was all it took, the man and his dog, who, by the look of it, should have been in a zoo and not a public park.

At this new danger I stuck close to Thomas.

115

After a little, as that he had weighed us up, the man rose from his bench and crossed over the grass and sat down beside Thomas. "How are you doing?"

"Okay."

"Is that your dog?"

"It is."

"What do you call him?"

"Martin."

"That's a strange name for a dog, Martin."

"Do you think?" Thomas appeared to be relaxed but I could feel the tension in him. The thick-set man in his string vest with a dog that was more than dangerous. I was far from cowed, but very wary. Showing my teeth at the other dog, and the man asked if I was a fighter?

"How do you mean, a fighter?"

"With other dogs. He's big and looks the goods to me." At this Thomas put me on the lead and I snarled back at the other dog who, all the while, had been snarling at me. "This one here, Tiger," the man said, "is the best fighting dog I've ever had."

"Then keep a fucking hold of him." But Tiger escaped or the man let go of his lead and, in a blink, the fight was on. It was the first real, as killing fight I had been in, and Thomas had dropped my lead in order that I could defend myself. This zoo-like creatures out to kill.

But I was far from scared and stood my ground. Tiger tried to seize my throat, but I was too quick – in truth he was rather cumbersome – and after he had missed my throat, I got his nose. A chomping bite that finished the fight and finished Tiger, who could fight no more without his nose. A big, blunt, pink-coloured snout and I could see the amazement in his eyes before he ran away to hide and die. That was the sort of fight it was, that one of us was mangled. I would doubt that Thomas saw all this, for he was busy exchanging punches with the string-vested guy, who had to be fucking nuts. First his dog and now himself, for he was caught with a punch that dumped him in the shrubbery.

I was, all of this, in such a frenzy that I would have bit out at anything, even Thomas, and it took him time to calm me down and bring me to my senses, to put my lead back on. "Let's go, Martin."

So, we got out of the park in, still, both of us, one piece or seemingly so, for, later, on the bus, I saw that Thomas had hurt his hand. But next stop Glasgow, home at last.

***

Thomas had more than enough of the loot for us to take a taxi from the bus station. The driver said not a word, his wild looking passenger and a big wild looking dog. We had been though the mill and it had to show and Mammy was shocked at the sight of the bedraggled, bearded, Thomas. "What happened?" She asked.

"I got drunk."

"At least you still have Martin."

"It's a miracle that I still have Martin." Thomas sat down in his chair. "Half of the time I did not know where I was."

Most of the time you did not know where you were.

Mammy said that he looked awful and he told her that he felt worse. "I didn't think we would make it home."

Neither did I.

Mammy made a cup of tea and asked about his hand. "It looks swollen to me."

Thomas said that he must have staved it when he was drunk, but, "I really can't remember." Then. "It won't happen again when we're away, I can tell you that."

"It shouldn't have happened at all," Mammy said. "Poor Martin."

"I'll make it up to Martin." Thomas ruffled my head. "It was a terrible time for Martin, too."

But I'm still here

"Was he fed at all?"

"I think a wee bit."

"How do you mean, you think a wee bit?"

"I might have fed him off and on and then forgot about it."

"I think you might have forgotten to feed him at all."

He did.

"He got something to eat this morning."

Mammy knew there was no point in scolding Thomas further and asked if he was hungry?

"I think we might both be a little hungry."

You're dead right there, because I'm fucking starving.

While Mammy was making food for him, he fed me with the dried food stuff that, for a time; my time in England, I had not thought to see again.

After our feeding – him with a much more tasty dish than I had had – we retired to our room and I slept on my couch and him in his bed and it was late at night, about three in the morning when he was awakened by my licking at his face, that I needed to go out.

Thomas did not complain and, when he was dressed, we went round to the hockey pitch where I did my business. and after that we had a walk about. He was still in the garb of a vagabond, which, I think, he had been mistaken for in the park in Birmingham where the man in the string vest had set his dog on me. "But it could have been worse, it could have been you," Thomas said. "You had no choice, Martin."

And that was true, the frightful Tiger who had been trained to kill to please his sadistic master. "A guy like that should be buried alive."

I agree.

"We'll try and put it behind us."

I already have.

Walking in the early morning, the moon and stars and it seemed to me like a new beginning. A change in Thomas that never again would he chance such peril, and, indeed, from there on in he was not drunk with me again.

Walking home from the hockey pitch Thomas held my lead with his left hand where it was usually his right. "I've got a pain in my hand, Martin."

This, the pain in his hand, would continue until, some days later, it was all discoloured and swollen up to twice its size, or even more.

This worried Mammy who urged that he should see a doctor. "It looks like it's infected."

"I was hoping that it would go away."

"It's becoming worse," Mammy said, "you're fingers are like sausages and you're wrist's all swollen too." Mammy went on to say that it was her guess that he had been bitten by an insect when he was drunk. "It's about the only thing that makes sense to me."

Mary agreed. "I heard about a man who had his ankle bitten by a cleg," she said, "and afterwards he lost his foot."

"Was this in Scotland?"

"In the Highlands."

"I was in the south of England."

"They might have cleg-like things in the south of England."

Thomas said he doubted that and that it was unusual for a cleg to inflict such damage.

"I'm telling you what I heard."

"I know, but it sounds pretty farfetched to me."

"Wait until you have a hook."

"Nobody has hooks these days."

"No, but you know what I mean; and that hand of yours needs medical attention."

Thomas agreed and said he would consult the doctor the following day. "I need to get it sorted out."

And he did. At the doctor's next day, he was sent to hospital where, and none too soon, a surgeon extracted two teeth out of this hand, his puffed-up knuckles.

He did not say to Mammy or Mary about the tooth. "We'll keep it a secret, Martin." Thomas with a bandage as big as a boxing glove wrapped round his hand. "It was all a nightmare, in that park in Birmingham."

***

Later that summer we were surprised to learn that Mark was

in prison, accused of assault. The love-sick man had, it seemed, attacked a woman who, he thought, had been having it off with Adam, who told Thomas that it was not true. "It was a friendship thing, and I told Mark that it was a friendship thing, but he wouldn't listen to me." Thomas was astounded by this news, a *woman*. "What happened?"

"He punched her face and broke her nose."

"That's awful."

"I cried all night after it."

"I always thought that he was jealous, but not of a woman," Thomas said. "It makes no sense."

"None at all," Adam agreed. "I don't fancy women."

And no woman in her right mind would fancy him, not physically. The guy was just too feminine, affected." Mark must be mad," Thomas said.

"As a hatter" Adam was in drag. In a blond wig and red lipstick and a bright blue summer dress. "She was a friend to me and Mark could not abide it."

Thomas shook his head and Adam went on, "Her name was Judy and she lived next door and we had been pals for ages. When I moved in with Mark, she was the first person to introduce herself and welcome me. As a friend, that is. She is happily married and I was flabbergasted when Mark suggested that we might be more than friends."

"When did this happen?"

"About a week ago. Something like that, and I am now moving out, away from here – it is Mark's house and he can do what he wants when he comes out of prison."

"When do you think that might be?"

"God knows, but hopefully not too soon." Adam was, as ever, holding Gigi, as clutching her to his bosom. "We were together for almost a year, but it's all over now, finally."

Thomas said that he had liked Mark, but could not condone his assault on a woman. "Not even if she was leading you on."

"You don't think that, do you."

"I don't know, but I've met some kinky women."

"What about *me*?"

"You could be kinky, too." This was the first time Thomas had been straight, direct with Adam who pretended shock. "I'm not like that at all."

"I only said you might be."

Watch out, Thomas; he could turn nasty, but he has a nice bare white leg for biting.

"Well, I'm not," Adam said. "At least not that way, with a woman."

Thomas said he didn't care, but he wished that Mark had

controlled himself

"Then that makes both of us." Adam bent down and kissed Gigi's little head. "Judy's nose is utterly ruined, and I hope that he gets years for it."

Thomas said it was serious stuff, if Judy's nose was as bad as that. "I take it that she was good looking before Mark got his hands on her?"

"She was," Adam said, "and her nose was her finest feature."

"He should have chastised you instead of her."

"What do you mean, have chastised me?"

Are you looking for a fight, Thomas?

"You must have known that your friendship with Judy would upset Mark."

"Not to that extent I didn't. That he would physically assault her. He's a dark one, Mark is, for neither one of us, myself or Judy, had the slightest inkling of what he had in mind."

"He might just have seen red, on the moment."

"No, he knew what he was doing, or going to do when she came to our door to ask my opinion of a new outfit she was wearing. But Mark answered the door instead of me and punched her face and broke her nose and blood was spewing everywhere." Adam touched his own nose with a long, red-pained fingernail. "It was awful, the whole thing. I heard the thud of the punch and the crunch of her nose." Adam shuddered. "It would have felled a bull, that punch."

"All this for nothing, or just his imagination."

"His imagination."

"What happened then, after he struck Judy?"

"He ran away, the dirty coward. I was left to try and calm her down and staunch the bleeding, but it was hopeless. She was in shock, and I can't blame her. You want to have seen the blood, Thomas."

Thomas

Adam went on to relate that he had alerted Judy's husband. He was only next door, after all. The husband could not believe his eyes at his stricken wife and turned on Adam. "I thought he was going to murder me."

"It was not you who did the damage."

"No, but he thought it was, or that I should have restrained Mark, and we don't talk any more. As for Judy, she is still in hospital and I don't know how I can face her when she comes out. The bridge of her nose is completely flattened, and she will never be the same again."

"Did you go with Judy to the hospital?"

"We both did, her husband and I. But I left before him. He is a big strong strapping fellow and I was taking no chances that he might turn on me."

"You must be shaken yourself, after such a happening."

Adam said he most certainly was. "I had to see the doctor, and I am now on Valium."

"I can't say that I am surprised."

Adam's beauty spot was somewhat smudged, for some tears had fallen on his cheek and he had wiped them off. "Later that night, after I had returned from the hospital, Mark came home and he was full of drink and we had a furious row and I called the police and he was arrested".

"You're lucky he did not go for you."

"Do you think?" Adam suddenly looked severe. "Don't let looks deceive you, Thomas."

"They don't."

"After what he had done to Judy, I could have scratched his eyes out."

"Did he try to explain himself or what?"

"He begged me to forgive him."

"You couldn't?"

"Could you?"

"I don't know – I mean, I feel sorry for Mark that he is in prison, but I don't like what he did to Judy."

"You don't *like*."

"The man is love-sick, Adam."

"Annabelle," Adam said. "My name is Annabelle when I am dressed up like a lady."

"That's no excuse."

"I think it is."

"Why are you sticking up for him?".

"I'm not."

"It sounds like you are."

"I only said that the man was love sick, and I'm sure he's sorry now."

"I bet he is," Adam said, "because I gave him quite a thrashing. He was in a pretty bad way when the cops arrived to pick him up, I can tell you."

Thomas frowned at this. "That was a cruel thing to do, to beat him up when he was drunk."

"It was no more cruel than what he did to Judy."

"If I was him, I'd break your jaw when I came out of prison."

"You would, would you?" Adam smiled in a challenging way, as a boxer might when touching gloves before the bell. "I'd like to see you try it."

***

"It was lucky that he was holding Gigi, or I think he would have gone for me."

I think so, too.

"I felt like punching *his* nose."

But it would have felt all wrong, like hitting a woman.

"Had he been less effeminate I would have done."

I think he might know that.

"If we see him again, we'll give him a swerve."

That would be wise.

"The problem is that I liked Mark."

I never much fancied either one of them.

"He's not a boy to cross, that Adam; I'll say that for him."

So, would I!

"Mark's safer in jail, away from him."

I agree.

***

That night with Adam – who escaped unscathed because of his dress, that it would have been too daft fighting a man who was dressed as a woman – was the last we saw of him. Thank fuck. A sensible Thomas who refused to fight, but if he was pressed too hard, he would. A mangled Adam. It was the only outcome. So, it was as well we did not see him. A sober Thomas. His drinking was now all but non-existent. The occasional slip, but nothing to worry about. On the romantic front there were no problems either. Some infrequent one-night stands that, if I disapproved because I missed him, I had learned to put up with. This long after his book had collapsed, fallen in. The publisher had been too small and his book was too unusual. So, Thomas thought, but he took it well, that, for all his hope, he had produced a dud. On the brighter side the same publisher – he could not find another, bigger one – had accepted a further novel, and a bit of a raise; an advance this time of five hundred pounds. A more realistic Thomas. "You would need to be awful lucky to get anywhere in this writing business, Martin." I was on my couch when he told me this, as a matter of fact; for he was far from down, just reflective. "If I was twenty years younger, I would go to Hollywood and try to become a screen writer." *What about me? We would have never met if you had gone to Hollywood. Better by far, for me at least, that you are a failed book writer*

"But I had no sense when I was in my thirties." We rubbed noses. The Eskimo kiss, as he called it. "I might have married a movie star if I had made my way to Hollywood."

It was times like this, on my couch; just him and me, that I liked especially. As a harp back to when I was a pup and had been sick and had thought to die and he had nursed me back to health. A long time ago. In the life of a dog as in another century. But I remembered it so clearly, the finest clarity. A first self-worth, and what I meant to Thomas. It was how I had felt when I was on my paws again. A new, unbreakable bond and if I had liked him before I loved him then and thank fuck, he had not gone to Hollywood. A script writer. Well, I do suppose that stranger things have happened. *Batman and Robin*. We had caught no bad guys, but we could hold our own if nothing else, and, together, it would have been the same in Hollywood. What fun and games with the movie people who, who knows, might have taken to a man like Thomas. But rather than there, in a glamorous California, we were on a couch in a council flat in Glasgow. "It was all a dream," Thomas said, "and the way it is, me and you, was how it was meant to be."

That was true. Me and him. Where we were and the way it was. On the couch in the room, my head resting in his lap. Precious moments. I should mention that Thomas did not advertise that he spoke to me, that was *our* secret. "A man is not supposed to speak to a dog, Martin."

I know that

"Some people might think that I am crackers."

Some people think you are already crackers, and they don't know you speak to me

"We've been pals for a long time now." Thomas in a pensive mood. Our friendship. And I can't state too much that we were equals. *Amigos*. I had never felt inferior, that I was less than him. This equality thing had been always there, something in his nature. That I was every bit as good as him, or maybe even better. It was the way he thought and that I was at the mercy of a hard, cruel world where the human was the master. It might be said, if it is not already obvious, that Thomas was none too fond of his fellow man and that, again, was to my advantage. What luck, or an inner instinct, that I had clutched on to the back of his hand and would not let go. No, sir; no way; and what an almighty joy when he paid whatever wherewithal and put me in his pocket. It was a lucky escape, for me at least; but what about my siblings. I had a sister, remember, who was kicked to death and, years later – after I had passed away – a Doberman dog was beaten to death in a Glasgow park, outside a toilet where it had been chained to a railing while its master was, supposedly, inside the toilet.

This was such a brutal assault that it was reported in a newspaper. The helpless Doberman had been set about by a group of youths who wielded golf clubs.

Thomas, when he read of this, was both saddened and enraged. That and a bit bamboozled, for the owner of the dog must have heard its screams as the golf clubs battered down on it. Had it been him and the dog was me he would have been out of that toilet in a flash and meaning fucking business. Not *that* owner. He had been too frightened. That was the long and short of it, that he had suffered his dog to save his hide.

The murderers were never caught, not; I don't think, that there was ever much of a hunt for them. The Doberman was only an animal, after all. To the world, but not to Thomas, who was moved to tears when he read the story – that it could have been *me*, that

Doberman – and he tried to track down the cowardly owner in the hope to catch the culprits. He was unsuccessful in his efforts, and knowing him and the rage he felt I was pleased of that. My old pal. He was getting on, too old for fighting; for taking on, what he would have done, a gang of vicious youthful thugs.

There are other, even worse incidents of torture in regards to dogs and I mention this one only because of the effect it had on Thomas.

Watching, looking on; I wished I was there to comfort him, but in the way of things that could not be and he had to bear with it alone.

There was a lot, after me, he had to bear alone, but that is not my story. I was not there, in the world, and far better that I cut it short, that revolting happening and his revulsion.

Earthly time. Who can understand it, time. It is an allotted space for every creature, and you can safely say that no dog will live to thirty-five or a man to be two hundred. Drear thoughts, or are they? In the span of space, and space is time, Methuselah is an infant. The trick, no matter how you look at it, is to enjoy your stay while you are still breathing.

Thomas and me, we enjoyed ourselves. Some ups and downs, especially; for me, when he met with women. The hateful Mrs. Smart for one. She is in her dotage now, in an old folks home and close, I think, to her last puff.

I will stay well clear of her and she from me when she puffs no more.

Thomas still has her gold watch for all, over the years, it has been in and out of pawnshops. Not that he gives a thought to Mrs. Smart or she to him for that matter.

But enough of this, such a hocus pocus, and a return again to the mortal world. On the couch where, as always – the Hollywood guff had been a complete one-off – he would repeat to me that he should have been a boxer. "But the booze put an end to that one, Martin."

It's about the only good thing booze ever did for you, I'd warrant

"Writing is a mug's game."

But it's the only thing that you can do!

"Four hundred pounds for a fucking novel, and I was lucky they accepted it."

I think you were, because it's a screwy book and no sensible man would have written it.

"I could have earned more for one fight on the undercard of a boxing bill."

You might have been carried out of the fucking ring, and you would have blown the money anyhow. You were never a cautious, wise man, Thomas.

"I might only have been a punch bag."

"Who knows?

"But I'd have made a lot more money catching punches than trying to catch words.

Yeah, sure!

***

In late September of that year, we went on another holiday. Another two buses, but much shorter journeys. The first bus went to Edinburgh and the second one on to Hexham, just over the English border. I would think about three hours in all, and we had Mary for company on our travels.

This time, rather than a lone caravan like the one we had in the seaside town, we were in a park that was full of them, caravans, and also had lots of people and dogs. But we kept to ourselves, and long walks and the caravan had two bedrooms and Mary slept in one while me and Thomas shared the other. I slept on the bottom and him on top and, when it was time to sleep, he would say, "Lights out, Martin," and the place was then in darkness.

It was all more civilized than our last adventure, and I was properly fed and Mary cooked breakfast for her and Thomas, who, as ever, let me steal a sausage or egg from off of his plate.

The weather was good, to begin with at least, and our walks took us into different towns and villages. As ever I stuck close to Thomas. Not that I disliked Mary, but it was always him I followed. Wherever he went I was never more than a step away, for, for all his faults – starving me in the seaside town - I was his and he was mine and that was how it had always been.

It was a good time, our time in Hexham; all the walking, and we stayed for a week and on our last day there, for a bit of a change, we boarded a bus to Newcastle with the intention of visiting Hadrian's Wall, that, as it turned out, was a fair distance from Newcastle. It was out of season and there was no bus service to take us there and so we had to walk. Down a long straight road that was named the Military Way. I would imagine the name had something to do with the Roman soldiers who had once manned the Wall. They must have been good walkers, for it had to be six miles at least from the city to their outpost. Not that it bothered us too much, not to begin with, before the rain began to fall.

The day till then had been dull and humid, a heavy low sky; and if I could sense the rain that was about to come, I could hardly tell them. No, and I would doubt that Mary knew about my secret talks with Thomas, or, more precisely, me listening in while he rattled on about this and that and a new young heavyweight named Mike Tyson.

I was off of the lead on the Military Way, because there was not a soul in sight. A sort of wasteland that, once the rain began to fall; as sheeted down, was turned into a quagmire. In all my life I had never seen such rain, a sheer torrent that blurred the vision and made you think of Niagara Falls or someplace very similar. I was drenched in a moment and my paws sinking in the quagmire. A jungle swamp!

There was really little difference, this deluge. It was enough for Noah to have clapped his hands in a wild delight. Not so Thomas and Mary who looked one to the other in disbelieve. On the Military Way with no place to shelter except, hopefully, Hadrian's Wall, that you could see in the distance, as wavering in the rain.

Thomas said, "This is fucking awful," and we, with me in the lead – I must have looked like some drowned rat – put on some pace to reach the Wall, some shelter from the pouring rain.

It was not to be, for what few shops were had closed, and there was only an open concourse. The Wall itself, all heavy stone; afforded no shelter, and we could only stand and brave the rain, that, by now, was fairly running out of us. I would think to have weighed; and my coat was short, ten pounds more than I had weighed before.

The rain had eased to a steady, heavy shower; but the damage was done and we were all soaking and in no mood to walk all the way back to Newcastle.

It happened then that a car drew up and a group of Japanese emerged from it. They were, one and all, some five of them, dressed in yellow hats and waterskins and with cameras around there necks. A vocal group, yattering away; and Thomas noticed that they had left their car unlocked and the key in the ignition. "What do you think?" he asked Mary.

"I think we should go for it."

We closed in on the car as the Japanese moved in closer to

the Wall. A feature of the Japanese, they appear; one and all, to have big buck teeth. And they showed them to us, in a show of rage, as Thomas drove their car in a sort of circle and out on to the Military Way.

I was in back with Mary in front, and she could not contain her laughter. The outraged Japanese. One of them, a tall man – or he was taller than the rest of them, who looked round and short – had run after us with his fist aloft. "If he catches you, he'll make you pay."

Thomas said he had no money.

"Money's the last thing on his mind."

"He won't catch me."

This was the first that I had been in a car with Thomas, and I was surprised by how quickly we were back in Newcastle. But I hoped that this, stealing cars, did not become a habit, because I much preferred to walk outside in the open air. But on the day, I was glad of it, and he parked near to the stop where the bus would take us back to our caravan. "That was a bit of luck," he said to Mary.

Mary said that it was funny. "You would have thought that they had seen a ghost when their car began to move."

Thomas said that he had only seen the tall guy who had shaken his fist at us. "I had some trouble with the clutch."

"I noticed that."

"It was the first time I've driven for twenty years."

"Thank God you did not stall."

"It was touch and go if I stalled or not, and I had to reverse the fucking thing."

"You shouldn't swear."

He always swears

Mary said it was the funniest thing, the astonishment of the Japanese and the tall guy chasing after us, that she had ever seen. "But we will need to keep it quiet."

"I suppose."

"Martin leapt straight into the back like he had been doing it all his life."

I had no intention of being left behind.

"He's soaked."

"So am I, and you are, too."

It was still raining, but more of a drizzle now. "We can change our clothes when we get back, but Martin can't."

"You think the world of Martin, don't you?"

He does

"He's my pal."

Mary said it would have not been so bad if they had had umbrellas. "We might even have walked it back if we had umbrellas."

"You would have missed a laugh if we had umbrellas."

Mary agreed that she would have done. "But I wish the bus would come, because those Japanese will find a phone and report the theft of their car by a man and woman and a big black dog."

This was – it's history now, isn't it? – before the days when two-year-olds had mobile phones.

Thomas said he had thought of that, if I would doubt he had, but, and it had to be his lucky day, for the bus came then and, for we returning home the following morning, there was little chance that the cops would catch us.

On the run back to our caravan Thomas said, "We only borrowed the car, that's all."

"And left *them* in the rain."

"The cops will have a good laugh at it."

"It's still a crime."

"But a funny one."

Mary agreed that indeed it was, had been. "I'll never forget the look of amazement on their faces."

"It'll be the talk of Tokyo, or wherever they come from."

***

Back in the caravan Mary made a meal and I was fed and afterwards, in a red-skyed night, we went out for a walk, a short one.

I think Mary phoned Mammy and there was a near-by green where I went with Thomas for a run about and to relieve myself before we returned to the caravan and, not long after, went to bed.

***

I yelped, cowered a little to make myself that little smaller and a harder aim for the snowballers. A group of boys who were across the street and who thought it fun to torment me. A captive target. I was tied to a post outside of the doctor's surgery. Not the first time I had been tied to this post while Thomas went inside to collect a prescription for Mammy. He was usually quick, just in and out, but was delayed that day because a man had taken a heart attack. In the meantime, I was hit again and again by the snowballers. *Hurry up for fuck sake, Thomas!*

The snow was thick on the ground and it was still falling. Big, slow, wafting flakes from out of a heavy, steel-like sky. There were people walking, passing by, but they paid no heed to me, my plight. I must have been hit by fifty, a hundred snowballs and, if I usually liked the snow, I hated it then, that day. As a dog in the stocks, it was how I felt, tied up and helpless.

When, finally, Thomas came out of the surgery, I was covered in snow and the snowballs still coming, crashing in on me. Thomas was not amused but he was prepared to let it go until, that was, I was hit by a stone wrapped up in snow. It hit my ribs and you could hear the crack and Thomas, who had seen the boy who had done the damage, was over the street in a flash. I'd warrant to have never seen him move so quickly. The boy, naturally, begun to run but he was too slow and Thomas kicked him on the arse. And I *mean* kicked. A swinging boot! It lifted him up into the air and then dumped him in the snow.

There were people who took a dim view of this, Thomas's chastisement, and he had to punch a man who protested in an abusive way. "You fucking bully."

It was hopeless to try and argue that it was the other way round, that the boy was the bully, and Thomas put the lead on me. "Are you okay, Martin?"

I wasn't really, but it was better by far that we were away from this place, where, over the street, there was a crowd of people around the boy.

"A fucking hooligan," Thomas said. "A kick in the arse was too good for him."

But he's still a minor, and the cops might come.

"If your ribs are sore rest assured that his arse is even sorer."

It was a good kick

"He'll think twice before he stones a dog again."

I don't think he'll ever stone a dog again We had cut through side streets to avoid perusal. "It's been a cunt of a day, Martin."

I know But I also knew that most humans are against a man who kicks a boy, however justly.

Thomas, for his part, felt self-righteous and, "I had to chin that guy or the whole pack of them would have been at my throat."

Without a doubt

"I won't tie you up again, Martin."

That's good news

"He was a cruel boy, hurting you for nothing."

You sorted him out

"I was fucking furious."

Dear, Thomas

When we got home, a somewhat hobble, I was able to eat my dinner, but, due to the pain in my ribs, I was none too lively.

"Is Martin okay?" Mammy asked. "He's not moving the way he usually does."

"He was snowballed when I was in the doctor's." Thomas sat and smoked and, I could tell, he was still angry. "A group of boys were hitting him with snowballs, and one of them threw a stone. I heard it hit on Martin's ribs, and I kicked the boy who had thrown it."

"How old was this boy?"

"About twelve, maybe thirteen. I don't know, and I was hardly caring."

Mammy was alarmed at this, because she knew Thomas and

knew that if he had kicked a boy, it was a fucking kicking. "You could get into trouble."

Thomas said he thought not, not now. That the matter was done and over with – what boy would admit to stoning a dog? – and, "He'll think twice before he stones a dog again."

"Do you think Martin might need to see the vet?"

"I hope not."

My rib's still hurting

"You could have been charged with child assault."

"He had no right to stone Martin."

"A court might think you had no right to kick him."

"It won't go to any court."

Mammy said she hoped it didn't. "Martin would hate it if you went to prison."

I'd die

Thomas said it was sheer bad luck that we had encountered such a boy. "I bet it's not too long before *he* is in prison."

I'd bite his arse if I got the chance

"Martin might have a broken rib."

"There's nothing much we can do about it even if he has. Maybe a few painkillers, but that's about all. Ribs usually heal up naturally, at least they do in humans."

"I hope he's not in too much pain."

Thomas said he might give me a couple of aspirins. "They won't do him no harm, but we'll see how it goes."

I'll heal, and I can do without the aspirins

Mammy said, "Poor Martin." Then, "I hope you did not hurt that boy too badly."

"I only kicked his arse." Thomas ruffled my head. "I don't think there's too much wrong with Martin."

But when Mary came home, she noticed straight away that there was something wrong with me, because I did not run to greet her as I usually did. "What's the matter with Martin?"

"He has a sore rib."

"What happened to him?"

Mammy said that a boy had hit me with a stone. "It was disguised as a snowball." She went on to explain that I had been tied up outside the doctor's surgery

Mary asked Thomas if he had caught the boy?

"I did, and I kicked his arse."

"You should have pulled out his teeth." *I'd liked to have seen that.* "It's what he deserved."

"He got a good boot in the arse."

He certainly did

"How old was he?"

"Young enough to be still at school."

"Were there any witnesses?"

"A few. But he should not have stoned Martin, and I only wish I had kicked him harder." And that was that. Thomas. He did not give a fuck, not really. The laws of the world, of humankind. "If that stone had crashed on Martin's head it could well have killed him."

Perish the thought

My ribs were sore for a few days, but I tried my best to hide the pain because I did not want to worry Thomas. Better by far that the whole affair was done and over with. A savage, brisk encounter that; and the first for years, since I was a pup and had first met Thomas, reminded me of my low station, that out with him, to the world at large, I was just a dog, a *cur*

***

"I wonder if Mark is still in jail?"

He might well be, if he broke a woman's nose

As time went on, Christmas and another year, a new spring, we forgot about him, so it was a big surprise when, right out of the blue, we met up again. "Where have you been hiding?" Thomas asked.

Mark smiled. His nose was bashed and his beard was white.

In the field above the city on a warm April night. "I think you know where I have been."

Thomas said he had some idea. "There's no point in kidding otherwise."

"But it's behind me now."

"That is good."

"And so is Adam."

"That might be even better."

Mark said he knew it was. "I spent a year in jail because of him."

What about the woman you hit?

"I was bewitched."

You must have been

Mark looked fit and well, because, I think, he was bewitched no more. His love for Adam who, it would seem, had dragged him down. His bashed-in nose and a year in jail. "But I have emerged from it a wiser man." Mark laughed. "At least I hope so."

Thomas said you live and learn and, "That's a nice wee dog that you've got there."

The wee dog, it was four or five months old, was black and white and wanting to play with me. But I was not in the mood to play with a pup and it got the message and left me alone.

"I picked him up from the dog rescue," Mark said. "He's only a wee mongrel, but I've already become quite fond of him."

"Has he a name?"

"Not yet."

"I think he might be a bit of a collie."

"So did they, at the dog rescue – but I'm not caring what he is."

"He's a big change from Gigi, I'll say that."

"Gigi belonged to Adam, and I only pretended that I liked her."

"You didn't?"

"No, but I had to pretend a whole lot of things when I was with him to keep the peace."

Thomas said he could believe that.

"I have a new man now, a chap I met in prison. His name is Freddie, and he's much more level-headed than Adam was."

"I would hope so," Thomas said, and went on to relate how Adam had faced him up. "He was spoiling for a fight."

"I don't doubt that, and he carries a hatpin with a six-inch needle, so you were more than fortunate that you were not stabbed."

Thomas shook his head, that he had not known about the needle. "But I always thought he was a dangerous young man."

147

"He was, and a lot more dangerous than you might think. Just look at my nose and how he has rearranged it."

He did that?"

"He did."

The bridge of Mark's nose was smashed, caved in, lending an upward tilt and a hog-like look."

"He mentioned that he had given you a thrashing."

"He did more than that, with a poker." Mark kidded to stagger on the grass. "Wham," he said, "and that was that and do you know what they called me in the prison?"

"No."

"Piggy."

"That was awful."

"I became used to it, and I do look like a trotter."

Thomas said he did not. "More unusual, I would think."

"I preferred the way I looked before."

So would I if I was you

"He said you were drunk when all this happened."

"I was, and he was quick to take advantage." Mark touched his nose. "The pity is I think now that the woman in question was only a friend, and I punched her face and went to jail for nothing, or only my imagination."

Thomas said he sympathized. "It's all about what love can do."

What about the woman he punched?

"I regretted it right away," Mark said. "I had never hit a woman before and I found myself in a frightful state. I mean, I think I knew I would get time for what I'd done, and I was terrified of prison, if, in the end, it was not too bad, most especially after I met Freddie."

"You haven't heard from Adam again?"

"No, not a word. But I have heard from some gay friends that he is in London and the sweetheart of a pop star."

"What about his lady friend?"

"She has moved away, both her and her husband, and we, Freddie and me, will soon be moving, too. None of the neighbours speak to us and we need a fresh start where we can put the past behind us."

Thomas agreed that so they did, need a fresh start, and they shook hands and we never saw Mark again.

***

Around this same time Thomas had his new novel published, and it proved to be another flop. But not the same blow this time around as he had suffered with the first. More, I think, he would have been astounded if he had been successful "I'm not caring, Martin."

But I think you are, a wee bit.

"My style is not commercial."

A fool could have told you that.

"I'm something of an outlaw in the laws of literature."

Are there laws in literature?

"You have to be awful good or awful lucky to fuck them up and get ahead."

"Then you should think to change your style if you want to be successful.

"I don't know where I go from here, because I'm tired of it all."

Take a break and think it over.

Thomas said he would do just that and he did not write another word for four years.

***

Our holidays were cheapies, outside of the disastrous one in the seaside town in the south of England. That had been a beezer, Thomas drinking all the wherwithall and then burgling a shop at night. My fight with Tiger in the park the following day in Birmingham. Thomas with a big black beard and a tooth embedded in his knuckles, if at the time he did not know it. Not that he could have done much about it even if he had. In the station, waiting for our bus to Glasgow. I had been more than glad to home from that one. We both were, and could well do without further such adventures. On holiday. This one was to Millport, a small island across from Largs which is a busy holiday resort on the west coast of Scotland. "I hope you are a good sailor, Martin."

By now I knew when we were going on holiday, because Thomas would pack my feeding dishes the night before. The one problem on our travels was that some people were frightened of me and would shy away. There was no need, for I was not about to bite some-one, but I was a Doberman, or supposed to be one, and Dobermans have a reputation as fierce dogs. This, while far from true (most Dobermans are of a placid disposition) has been helped along by books and films such as THE BOYS FROM BRAZIL where, in a horrific scene, Gregory Peck is mauled to death by a pack of them.

This film was shown on late night television and me and Thomas watched it. The Dobermans were purportedly owned by a schoolboy Adolf Hitler who was delighted to see Gregory being ripped apart.

The biggest of the Dobermans was named Ketchup and it was obedient to Hitler, who was a very cruel boy. What else would you expect? Gregory, for his part, was a German doctor who, we were led to believe had cloned the Fuhrer and, this was in America, had come to tell him of his great mission. But Hitler thought that he was insane, and that was the end of Gregory. It was an entertaining movie, if a bad advert for Dobermans, and it is because of that and other fiction that we are viewed as dogs to watch, to beware off. One the train on the way to Largs I was eyed suspiciously by some of our fellow travellers. It was nothing new and I simply yawned, ignoring them. Thomas, too, was used to it, the alarm of strangers who, who knows, might well have seen THE BOYS FROM BRAZIL. There were plenty of dogs on the seafront at Largs, where Thomas kept me on the lead. On the promenade, for the beach was full of pebbles. "I sometimes wish you were a poodle, Martin." *A poodle would not have suited you.*

And neither it would, because Thomas was a big strong man who needed a big strong dog. He was the sort of guy who would have looked stupid with a poodle. It just was not him, the man he was, and, certainly, right from the first, from the moment I had clutched on to his hand and would not let go, it was in the stars that we were meant to be together.

It is a short, a ten-minute sail from Largs to Millport, but, on arrival, you are in a different world. There are few cars in Millport, but lots of bicycles. It was, as we would discover, a bicycle, the main mode of transport on the island. That or walking, what we would do, for no-place is far in Millport. It is a tiny, like stamp-sized island, and when we found our caravan – it was one of eight – there were lots of people and a number of dogs and all of them loose, running free, and I could have joined them if I had wanted too, but I could not be bothered.

The main joy of our caravan holidays was, as said, that we slept together, in the same bed. Sometimes Thomas overslept because he had been reading a book until the early hours. Not that I cared for I was becoming that little older and was all for oversleeping too. The only problem was at breakfast time when Thomas ate a cereal and I had no fried egg to steal. A small thing, but I was used to it and I missed my morning egg. Against that we had the open air and fantastic walks and on one of the days we encountered a guard goat.

This was a large, lean, staunch animal that stood up to me when I growled at it – it was lucky that Thomas had seen it first and had put me on the lead – and would not let us pass.

The goat had been guarding sheep, but they were now penned up and it had taken to guarding the gate. This was on a narrow, lane-like road and we had to climb over a short stone dyke and into a field to pass it by.

"That goat should be on a rope or something," Thomas said. "Did you see its horns?"

They were not that big.

"One kick from its hoof would have smashed your ribs."

I'd have been too quick.

"But it's got courage, I'll say that for it."

So, have I.

"It thought it was doing its job, was all."

It was a big thing with Thomas, in man or beast, that they could stand up for themselves. Had we met with a brave mouse he would have turned around and walked away rather than a show of force to demean the creature. Thomas had a lot of faults, but he could not abide a bully. Mrs. Smart. He had been fond of her, if I can't think why, until she began to bully him, that it was her or me, when, with a little more sense, it could easily have been both of us. Ho awful, sharing him with a thing like her. But I would have had no choice except to play along. I was only a dog, after all, as Mrs. Smart was not slow in reminding Thomas. She was wrongly named, was Mrs. Smart, for, all in all, she was not smart at all. Not that Thomas was much smarter, for he could, and should, have taken her for a whole lot more than just a watch. But, and for a man like him who was none too honest, he had a queer sense of honour that had forbidden him to take advantage of her. As it was, he was full of praise for the guarding goat that had showed a wealth of courage. We did not encounter it again because Thomas avoided where it was. "There's no point in looking for trouble, Martin."

Later that day in the caravan park we encountered a young woman who, to coin a phrase, was as black as coal. She was the first coloured person I had met and I got along okay with her. Her name was Lizzie and she had come to Millport to get away from a troubled romance. "Someone in London suggested it."

"I'm surprised that someone in London had even heard of it."

"She is Scottish."

"That figures."

"She was brought up in Largs."

"Where were you brought up."

"Jamaica. My family came to Britain when I was five."

"That can't have been too long ago."

"Twenty years."

Thomas said she did not look her age, "Or anything like it."

Lizzie said she had been in Millport for the best part of a week and this was now her last three days.

She was in the caravan next to us and, "I hope that you're not scared of dogs."

"I'm not." She looked down at me. "What's his name?"

"Martin."

"My boyfriend's name is Martin, too."

"That's a strange coincidence."

"I know, but you don't get too many dogs named Martin, do you?"

"No, you don't."

"What are you doing here?" Lizzie asked. "I mean, it's remote."

"I know, but it suits me. It's not every caravan park that accepts dogs, and I felt like a break.

"Things were beginning to get to me, so I thought for a bit of peace and quiet." Then, "My name is Thomas."

Thomas appeared to get along with Lizzie and they agreed to meet the following morning for a walk. "I bet she has a story to tell," Thomas said in the caravan that night. "A young girl like her coming to a place like this."

I think the same.

I was not jealous of Lizzie because, whatever happened, it could only be a brief affair, a one off. There is a big difference between that and an ongoing thing like with Mrs. Smart.

Lizzie was dressed in white shorts, the better to show her long smooth black legs that appealed to Thomas who had high hopes that, and soon, he might be more than friends with her. The main problem was their ages, she being much the younger, and he did not want to push it. It was better for him to play the older – but not too old – well-meaning gentleman in the hope that she would come on to him.

During our walk Lizzie burst into tears. "I'm sorry, Thomas."

Thomas said it would do her good. "We all cry sometimes to relieve the tension, Lizzie."

I've yet to see you cry.

There were various wayside cafes and we stopped at one that had gaily painted tables outside "It's good luck for me that I met you," Lizzie said. "It's no fun to be alone."

"None at all, and I've been lonely myself since I came to this place."

"But you've got Martin."

"I have, but I still like human company."

Especially a woman's!

Sipping her coffee Lizzie declared that she was a singer. "Not that you will have heard of me."

"No?"

"I sing in clubs, that's all."

Thomas said his favourite singer was Shirley Bassey and that Lizzie looked a bit like her. "When Shirley was young, that is." Lizzie said she was blacker than Shirley by at least ten shades and Thomas was the first person to suggest they looked remotely alike. "Personally, I can't see it."

"You have a better figure."

"I'm fuller."

"You certainly are."

"My bum's too big."

Thomas smiled and shook his head. "Don't be daft, it's perfect."

An odd thing, or so I thought; my dog's nose, there is a

distinct smell –difference between a white person and a black one. Why this should be I do not know, but it is a fact. Saying that Lizzie smelled nice, young – yes, you can tell a person's age by their smell – and fresh and full of sap.

"Are you trying to flatter me?"

"I'm telling you the truth, that's all."

Lizzie said it was nice to know that Thomas thought she had a perfect bum. "But I don't."

"But you do, take it from me." After such a compliment Thomas asked what sort of songs she sang.

"Rap, usually; a bit of jazz. I don't think you would like, it if you liked Shirley Bassey."

"I liked Vera Lynn, too."

"How old are you?"

"I'm in my forties."

"Vera Lynn must be ninety if a day, and Shirley Bassey's no spring chicken, either."

"I know, but I like their singing."

"What about more modern singers?"

"Cliff Richard."

"He's a good age, too." Lizzie looked at Thomas. "I wouldn't have taken you for a fan of Cliff Richard."

"I'm not, not really; he just came to mind, but he is a good singer."

"If you like his singing, but I don't – I think he's just an old fuddy duddy."

"I don't know too much about modern singers."

"That's obvious." Lissie sort of rolled her eyes. "Vera Lynn, she's some fucking time ago."

I was surprised to hear Lizzie swear, but that is modern women for you.

"I've listened to her records, that's all; White Cliffs of Dover and all of that."

"I think you are an old-fashioned man, Thomas."

"I suppose I am, in the music business, anyhow."

"Let's talk about something else."

"You're bum?"

"No, not my bum."

"What, then?"

"You. What do you do, work at?"

"I'm a writer – not that you would have heard of me, either."

"What do you write?"

"I've written a couple of novels, but they got nowhere."

"Then you will need to write another one, won't you?

"That is easier said than done."

"What were they about, you're novels?"

"The Glasgow slums back in the fifties."

"Did you come from one, a slum?"

"I did. The Gorbals."

"I think that I have heard of it, the Gorbals."

"It used to be famous, or infamous."

"Is it a tough place?"

"Not now, but in the fifties it was, when we still had the old tenements."

"There are some tough places in London, too."

"I'm sure."

"My boyfriend is a gangster."

"I've known a few."

"You have?"

"I have."

"He's the leader of the gang. The Huba-Huba they call themselves, and it's only a matter of time before they kill someone."

"This is the Martin guy that you were telling me about?"

"It is."

"Is he black?"

"As a berry. His family is from Jamaica, the same as mine."

"Where did you meet him?"

"In a club where I was singing. Everyone was scared of him and it was a big thing when he asked me out.

Thomas said that a lot of girls fell for gangsters. "But it beats me why." Lizzie said that it might be glamour. "They have a certain swagger, and are larger than life."

"Is that the reason you fell for him?"

"That and he's six foot six and he made a great big fuss of me."

"How old is Martin?"

"Twenty=nine."

"Isn't that a little bit old for running in a gang?"

"It's organized. They're not street thugs. It's all about money and they're into almost everything, protection and drugs and prostitution."

"He sounds quite a guy, this Martin."

"Are you surprised?"

"A little. I didn't think you would have anything to do with a guy like Martin."

"Neither did I. It just came about. He can be really, really loving; but he has a mean streak, too."

"He would hardly be a gangster unless he had."

"He has asked me to marry him."

"Will you?"

"I don't know. That's the reason I came to this place, to try and think things out."

Thomas said from the sound of it he'd steer clear of Martin. "I like a quiet life."

Lizzie said she was half in love and half in fear of Martin.

"Try to forget all about him until you return to London."

Lizzie said that she would try. "But it's not fucking easy."

***

"A gangster's moll," Thomas said. "I would never have taken her for that."

Nor me.

"She seems much taken by this man, but she's scared of him too."

I know she is, but he is far away and she is here in Millport.

"She's all at odds about the guy."

If *she had any sense, she'd dump him.*

***

162

"Did you sleep well, Lizzie?"

"Like a log."

"So did I. It must be all this country air."

Lizzie was wearing long pants, but they were tight and bright, a dazzling pink, and she had to know what she was doing to Thomas, who, still, was determined to play the gentleman. For as long as he could with a girl, who, as warming to him, took his hand. Walking. We went a different way and stopped at a different café where, again, they had a coffee and Thomas gave me a biscuit. A McVitties digestive. He bought packet once a week and treated me at random. Sometimes half a biscuit. A mean Thomas. He thought I did not know the difference between a half biscuit and a whole one?

Well, Thomas, I have news for you, I did.

Lizzie in a white short-sleeved shirt that clashed with the blackness of her skin, her arms. They were rather hairy, but rather than off-put that excited Thomas, who said, "I really like you, Lizzie."

"I like you, too."

So far so good, the hesitant Thomas. But not too hesitant. A holiday romance is of necessity brief, and you can't waste too much time. "Don't you think it strange that we met up, that we both came to Millport at the same time and to the same caravan park."

Lizzie said she had been about to say the very same thing. "You took the words right out of my mouth."

"I was thinking about it last night, that it must have been fate that we met up."

Lizzie agreed. "I wasn't looking for companionship when I came to Millport."

Liar, you always have an eye open for a pretty woman, and some not so pretty.

"Yet here we are together," Lizzie said, "just like old friends."

"We get on together, don't we?"

"Have you been to London, Thomas?"

"I have. I worked down there for a few months back in the sixties."

"That's a long time ago."

"It certainly is, but we had the Beatles and Stones –you must have heard of them."

Lizzie said she loved the Beatles music. "Especially the White Album."

Thomas who had never been into music and had never heard of the White Album, declared it was a masterpiece. "You don't get music like that today."

Lizzie said she wouldn't say that. "But it was brilliant stuff."

So, it went. This and that, and all the time, from the first, Lizzie had no illusions about his friendship.

You want to seize the bull by the hours, Thomas.

Still, he had practice enough and had to know what he was doing. Strangers in Millport. I was surprised he had not mentioned Frank Sinatra. A bit of an oldie but a more upbeat choice that Vera Lynn. I can't think of any singer less upbeat than Vera Lynn.

When they were walking again, they were much closer, almost hip to hip, and she was willing and more than willing and trusting Thomas for the gentleman he was supposed to be. And I suppose he was. With women. It was part of him, the way he was. Nothing forceful. Not at all, and I noticed his hand touching Lizzie's arse, and she was not complaining. Back in the caravan I was locked-up while Thomas went to visit Lizzie, in her caravan. But a short session. A couple of hours, if that. "I didn't want to leave you for too long, Martin."

How did it go?

"She's a beautiful woman," Thomas said. "I was lucky to have had her."

She's bored, that's why you had her

"Her heart's in the right place."

I think I already knew that.

"She's a bit mixed up, but aren't we all?"

I'm not.

"Anyhow, I've no complaints, and I don't think she has

either."

Then good for you and Lizzie.

"She's half my age or even younger. I am the oldest guy she has been with."

You're hardly Methuselah.

"There's no future or anything, but we enjoyed each other."

And they would enjoy each other again the next day. Another couple of hours. I did not mind, not at all, for in my dog sense and knowing him I knew it was a one-off fuck, that she was too young or he was too old and when they parted – Lizzie back to London – he would soon forget her, and she him for that matter.

***

Back in Glasgow we began to frequent Kings Park. It was about a mile away, me on the lead; for we had to walk on streets, but well worth it when we got there. It is a large park, King's Park. We went in though a long walkway where I would run in front and, sometimes; in the hope to bamboozle me, Thomas would hide behind a tree. But I always found him and one of the days, when I did, I knocked him down in welcome. A sprawled-out Thomas. He had to have been caught off balance, but it was all fun. In this park we met two young boys who, between them, had a Boxer and a Collie. They were the happiest boys and their dogs were happy too. Playful and full of fun. The boys, they were about fourteen, came from large, bought houses and were polite and well brought up. A good happy company that was to be ruined when a pit-bull – something like the dog I had fought in the park in Birmingham – killed the Boxer for no reason at all.

We were not there when this had happened, or it would not have happened, and we wondered if it was the same pit-bull that had savaged the Snauzer some time back. There was no way of telling, not for certain, but I think it was. There are few dogs, even of the bull terrier breed, who will kill another dog for no reason. When Thomas enquired about this dog, he was told that it had been taken away from its abode before the police arrived to investigate the incident. We were, especially me; because I had come to know the Boxer, what was a gentle fun-loving creature, upset about this, that it should meet its end in the jaws of a bull terrier, that had had to be trained and encouraged to kill.

Thomas said if he met the owner he would break his jaw, and that was very true.

I was glad to see, some weeks later, that the boy had acquired a new Boxer pup that appeared to be of the same good disposition as its predecessor.

There were plenty of dogs and walkers in Kings Park, and we met with an ex-policeman that Thomas knew. Indeed. He was one of the cops who had come to our door after I had bitten his colleague. They had a good laugh about it and no ill-will and his name was Harry and he had a huge Rotweiller that was well able to take care of itself.

This dog, Nelson, was a good play-mate and Harry kept an eye on him in case our play got out of hand.

The same could be said for Thomas, who, to begin with, had been a bit leery of Nelson, given his huge size.

But there was never any trouble, and I liked to meet with Nelson and Thomas liked to meet with Harry, who, on that long ago night had gone out of his way that I was spared after the outraged cop had punched Thomas on the eye. "It was the easy way out for all of us," Thomas said, "that he lost his temper."

Harry agreed. "I would have felt really bad to have had Martin put down for a dangerous dog."

"There was no way that would have happened."

"Not if it wasn't Martin, as you claimed," he laughed.

"But he accused Martin."

"He did that," Harry agreed. "And he was bragging about the punch he hit you with for years after."

"It was worth the punch."

"That's what I thought."

"I heard that someone slipped him a horse laxative sometime later."

"Someone did, and he almost died. I think he was a couple of days in intensive care, and he was never the same man afterwards."

"Did they catch the culprit?"

"No." Harry shook his head, a wry smile. "It was the talk of the station, but whoever did it wasn't saying,"

Thomas said he had thought it funny. "But then I had never liked the guy."

"Did you see him again, after that night?"

"Once or twice, but I tried to keep out of his way."

Harry was a tall, slim man who, before he had joined the police, had spent time in the army. "I must like uniforms."

Thomas said he hated them. "They're usually trouble, one way or another."

"It was only a job," Harry said, "in the army or in the police. At least it was to me if, again, you get over zealous cops who are too quick with the handcuffs.

"Saying that you need handcuffs for the job, because there are people out there who would carve you up as quick as winkie."

That was a new word to me, winkie.

Harry was low-key, but with a laconic sense of humour. "Had you seen some of the victims you would be horrified."

"The policeman's lot."

"It can sometimes be a sorry one."

Thomas agreed, about the policeman's lot, and asked Harry how he had come by Nelson.

"In the dog rescue. Nelson had been ill-treated and was a bag of bones and my heart went out to him."

"He's not thin now, and he looks to be in the best of health."

"He is. But he has had a terrible past, believe me."

We met with Harry and Nelson two or three times a week, and, whatever his past, Nelson was bright eyed and keen and boisterous with the best of us. The dogs in the park. There were children too, for the park was positioned near to two schools, and, as children will, both boys and girls, they would sometimes ask about me and Nelson.

This did not trouble Thomas, but Harry had a definite aversion to our young admirers. He had a reason for this, because when he had been a policeman, two young girls had accused a man of a serious sexual offence. It was supposed to have happened in a park when the man was out walking with his dog. "Their story was perfect down to the smallest detail, and we had no option but to arrest the man.

"He appeared in court the following day and was remanded into prison

"Needless to say, his family was told and his wife left him."

How old were the girls?"

"One was eleven and the other twelve. They were a picture of innocence and it was hard to believe that they had made the whole thing up

"As I said they described it all in fine detail."

"I take it that the man denied the charges?"

"He did. But it was two against one, and he had been in the park at the same time as the girls.

"There was nobody, including me, who had the slightest doubt that he was guilty. Everything fitted, and we had police women – experienced detectives – who had interviewed both girls individually. In different rooms. They stuck to their story all the way, in every detail."

"Did they have something against this guy?"

"I don't think so. Not that I know off, anyhow. They had spoken to him a couple of times, but otherwise he was a complete stranger and they did not even know his name or where he lived

"Anyhow, we were soon at his door, and, to tell the truth, were quite rough with him. A lot of cops have young children and nobody likes a sex offender, which we thought he was.

"I was in the station when the girls first made their accusation, and I have to say that I felt no pity for him."

"Were the girl's parents there when they reported this allegation?"

"Their mothers were." Harry smoked a pipe and took a long inhale. "They were respectable women, who believed their daughters, as we all did at that time." Then, after a pause. "I don't need to tell you we were wrong."

"Did the guy get out of prison?"

"He did. He had only been in for a week or so, but long enough to have lost his wife and children. Mud sticks, and she – his wife – would have nothing further to do with him."

Thomas said it would have been bad enough a week in jail, "But losing his wife and family, too."

Harry said the last he heard was that the man had become a hobo. "A wine drinking tramp."

"And all for nothing."

Harry puffed his pipe. "I still can't credit those two girls, they looked like butter wouldn't melt in their mouths."

"How did you find out they were lying?"

"The younger girl confessed to her mother that it was all a hoax, and the mother brought her to the station.

They were in a flood of tears, both of them, and it didn't take much for the girl to confess that they had made the whole thing up."

"Why do you think they did that?"

"It might have started a sort of dare that had went too far, that they were all caught up and couldn't confess that it was all lies. I don't know. But it was enough for me not to speak to children."

Thomas said, after hearing this story, that he would think twice before he spoke to children in the park. "It would destroy me, such an allegation."

"Me, too," Harry said. "It was all a long time ago, but I can't forget it, how we swallowed the whole thing, what he was supposed to have done to them."

"It wasn't rape?"

"No, and they never claimed that – I suppose they knew that it would have been too easy for us to have proved otherwise – but attempted rape is another story."

"What did the mother say about this whole affair, an innocent man imprisoned?"

"That she was sorry. The damage had been done, and a man had lost his reputation. You know, no smoke without fire. There were people who thought the worst of him."

"So, you are not for taking chances?"

"I am not. What happened to that guy was warning enough for me not to speak to children.

Thomas said he did not blame him. "I would never have though that such a thing could happen."

"It happened okay," Harry said. "And those two girls would have fooled Sherlock Holmes, I can tell you."

***

"A horrible story that one, Martin."

You don't speak to children, no-how.

"I wonder what happened to the girls?"

You should have asked.

"I bet they got away with a warning."

So, do I.

"They should have been horse-whipped."

I agree.

"Imagine he was one of the cops who came to our door after you had bitten his mate."

That was fucking years ago and I've bitten no-one since.

Speaking with Thomas. It had long become the most natural thing and I somehow knew what he was saying. How, why? I was only a dog, four paws and a tail – or the stump of one – and I could not talk, for all I wished sometimes I could.

At the time I thought nothing of it, and I thought other dogs understood the human tongue much the same as me. I know better now, but that was the way it was for us, if I don't think Thomas knew I knew what he was saying, not, I don't suppose, that he cared too much. No. It had become as normal that we would converse, with Thomas doing all the talking.

***

My play with Nelson was becoming rough, an almost fight, and he had begun attacking other dogs. This was a blow to Harry, who blamed Nelson's past, but, and try as he might, he could not stop it. I witnessed one assault, when Nelson went for an Irish Setter. It was a well-groomed much-loved pet and the woman who was in charge of it screamed and screamed as the Setter was almost mauled to death. Harry got out of that one by paying vet fees and by begging the woman to let it go. But there was no controlling Nelson, who, for whatever reason, had turned rogue overnight. One of the days, according to Harry, he had jumped on the back of a poodle, flattening it, and it was only cash that had saved the day for Nelson.

"Three hundred pounds," Harry said, "it had a broken rib and there were other, smaller injuries."

Thomas took a dim view of this behavior, and, "You'd better watch out, Martin."

"Harry's at his wits end."

You would be too, if it was me instead of Nelson.

"I wonder what is wrong with Nelson?"

His head, you fool.

"I think that Harry should have him to a vet."

I agree.

"It's something more than his bad past."

Maybe not. He might have been hit on the head when he was a pup and some underlying damage.

Nelson was okay when he was on the lead and, of late, in the park, he was always on the lead.

For myself, this new aggressive Nelson, I stayed well clear. There is a difference between braveness and foolishness and it would have been a foolish dog that mixed with Nelson.

But, too, it was sad; the huge Rottweiler who, after a dreadful start in life, had found a new, devoted owner. Which Harry was, if, really, he should have had him receive medical attention.

As it was, both man and dog were getting a bad name. Even me and Thomas, had begun to shun them. "I don't want you to be fighting, Martin."

Neither do I, because Nelson was my pal.

"We'll keep well away from them."

And so, we did and so were not there when Nelson turned on Harry, who dropped the lead, freeing the big Rottweiler who then attacked a German Shepherd.

The Shepherd stood up for himself, inflicting bites on Nelson, but in the end, it was no match for the Rottweiler who, after he was done with it, ran away as fast as his legs would carry him.

By then Harry had recovered from the assault on him and went in search of Nelson. He had a bite on his hand that would require stitches, but he was not for letting that hold him back. Nelson might attack and kill a child as easily, or more easy, as he had killed the Shepherd. It was a matter of urgency that he found Nelson, which he did. The big Rottweiler was under a bush and as docile as could be.

What Harry intended to do with Nelson I don't know, but I would suspect to have him put down. What else? Anyhow, he put the lead on Nelson who, after his fit of madness, was queerly subdued and not a little shame faced. The big Rottweiler. He had lost an ear in his fight with the Shepherd and was bleeding profusely. And so was Harry, his bitten hand. What a sad end for both of them, and worse; for Nelson suddenly collapsed and died. He was too big and much too heavy for Harry to even attempt to carry, so, and check that he was really dead, he covered the body as best as he could and went away to call for help, and, later, he buried Nelson in his garden.

I was really sorry to hear of this, the end of Nelson, who, it turned out, had died of a brain tumor.

***

A bit about me, my four-legged self, for by now I was more than nine years old. This is a long, long time in the life of a dog and I had a touch of arthritis and some stiffness in my joints. Not that I was falling down, far from it; but, let's say, I was not the dog I used to be. A more stilted, slower me, where I had once been loose and quick as a flash. I was aware of this and accepted it, for what else could I do? At this time, in 1991, I had lost some teeth and there was white in my muzzle but I was still on my paws and Thomas closed his eyes to my decline, if, knowing him, he had to be concerned, or, with a bit more accuracy, downright fucking worried. His old pal, and I was all of that; nine years together, his old pal. *Nothing lasts forever, Thomas.* At this time, Mammy was declining too. When I had first arrived, she had been old, or so I thought, perhaps because of her white hair. But she had been sturdy enough and energetic. She had had to feed and clean up after me, remember. I had been fond of Mammy ever since, and, in truth, she had kept the house together. But that was then and this was now and Mammy in her eighties. A more pale, fragile look. For all of that she still insisted to do the cooking. Thomas's breakfast, and mine. But a definite shuffle and her back was bent and she had lost a lot of weight. Thomas must have seen this too and it was another worry, his mother. But what to do? You can't fight age but you can close your eyes – as Thomas did, for he did not want to lose her – and pretend it is not happening.

There was nothing wrong with Mammy's head, and she retained a good sound common sense and she could count her money to the penny. But old age does not come alone and rather than walk she was beginning to stagger, and this was really sad to see.

Mammy was not five foot tall, but she had a big heart and the day had begun as any other with her cooking up the breakfast. I stole my share as usual, and a little later we, Thomas and me, went out for a while; for an hour at best, and when we returned Mammy was a cripple, a stroke victim.

It transpired that she had gone out to a local shopping van

where, while buying messages, she had collapsed and had to be carried back inside the house. But it did not seem too bad a stroke, not at first, for she was sat in her chair and quite composed and compos mentis. Against that she had lost the power in her right side and her mouth was twisted, and when the doctor came – I was locked in the room for fear that I attacked him – he was not slow in calling in an ambulance. Thomas went in the ambulance with Mammy and I was left in the house alone. It was horrible, the whole thing; and all so sudden, the doctor and the ambulance and Mammy carried out, away, and I whimpered and cried and wished that Thomas would come back soon.

It was not to be, not that day. The month was March and it was cold and a chilliness in my heart. In the house, and I was not used to this, to be in the house alone. What on earth – and I use that word advisedly – was happening? The daylight went to darkness and still no Thomas and I could sense the life we had had for many years was over.

When, finally, Thomas returned he was down in the dumps and I, knowing this, was down in the dumps as well. The missing Mammy who, in a way, our little group, had held it all together.

Thomas took me round to the field and I was fed on our return. Not that I had much of an appetite. The day weighed on me, and I was fearful of the consequences for a sombre Thomas. I licked his face in the hope that I could comfort him, that he was not alone in his despair, in this, by far, the biggest crisis he had faced. The missing Mammy. I hoped somehow, she would reappear, as walk in through the door. It was not to be and Thomas hardly slept a wink that night and, in the morning, he went out and I was left alone again.

I had to do without him for the remainder of that day, as he could not take me to the hospital where Mammy was. That fucking stroke. It had turned our whole world upside down. In the days to come I was left on my own for hours on end and Thomas, when I saw him, was totally dejected. "I don't know if she'll live or die, for she is in a bad way, Martin."

So am I, stuck in the house alone all day and I'm really frightened about what has happened.

"She'll never be the same again, that's for sure."

No, she wouldn't; and neither would we, for she had always been there, in the house, since I had arrived all those years ago. They had gone so fast, eight, or was it nine, Christmas'? Thomas and Mammy at mid-night mass, and I had loved it when they had returned and we, me and him, had gone out in the early morning. One thing about Thomas, he had been energetic then. I didn't know about now, for Thomas had changed drastically since Mammy had her stroke. A lot of spirit had gone out of him and I had the impression that he, too, was becoming old: as that all the worry about Mammy had aged him prematurely. He was, whatever way I looked at it, not the man he had been before. As full of his own mortality, and that meant for both of us. This staying alone in the house all day had a woeful effect on me, on my spirit, that, in a way, I was loved no

more. All his attention was on Mammy and how, in the hospital –
where he went each day – she was getting on.

She would be in hospital for a long time, Mammy. From
March to September, and in that period, I progressed from late
middle aged to old. Nothing, not yet, at the critical stage, but I had
lost a lot of fluidity. The easy trot I used to have, I would never know
again. That this was age I did not know, not then; and it would have
made no difference if I had, for there was nothing could be done
about it.

***

When Mammy came home, I hardly knew her, for she was a
very different person. An effigy of the woman she'd been, all
shrivelled up and, in a wheelchair, and, as I would soon discover, far
from being alone all day, I now had too much company. A relay of
nurses who, some of them, were scared of me and I had to be locked
up before they would cross the threshold. Thomas had, it would
seem, brought Mammy home against the wishes of the hospital and
she was in a much worse state than he had thought. We had a
hospital bed and a commode and a special chair that, after the nurses
had gotten her up, she would sit in all through the day and into
evening, until the nurses put her to bed again.

Poor Mammy, she had not deserved to come to this; a
complete cripple with only the use of her left arm and hand and all
confused and totally dependent on the visits of the nurses. They
came three times a day and Mammy like a rag doll, from her bed to

the chair and back again and, for she had always been so independent, this was very, very sad.

Usually, though, when the nurses were there, we, me and Thomas, would go out for a walk and when we came back the nurses had gone and Thomas would try to spoon-feed Mammy a cereal. It took forever for she would drool and he had to wipe away the excess of food. This woman who smelled like Mammy. She certainly did not look like her. In her chair, as helpless as a baby. But Thomas was encouraging and said she would get better. "Wait and see."

Mammy shook her hear. "I think this is the end of me."

"Don't say that."

"Look at the state I'm in."

"We will make out, we always have."

But Mammy did not believe it, him; who was the author of this, of bringing her home because he thought – or had thought before – that she would improve in familiar surroundings. "That hospital nearly killed you."

"It was the stroke that nearly killed me." There were times, even then, when she had more sense that Thomas, who, for all of that, had to know that this was one fight that he had no chance of winning.

A stroke is a brain injury and Mammy had small memory since the moment it had struck her. The good thing was, for her at least, that this was not – how could it be? – a worry, no, and in a way, it was a blessing that she could not remember the aftermath of that frightful day and the subsequent indignities she had been through. There were other changes, mind-wise, like, for one, that her memory was phenomenal for events of long ago. A distant past as bright as day, from when she had been a child. This astonished Thomas, if he wished she could remember more, short-term; what day it was, for instance. It was a complete blank. She was all at odds, was Mammy. The work of her head. At times, as illustrated, that it was the stroke that had almost killed her, she was more than lucid, then, as some click in her head, not a word of sense for days. The worst days of my life by far, and I was fast deteriorating. It was now a task to do the toilet, as my hind legs would not support me and I would sometimes fall back down into the mess. Thomas would help me up and wipe me clean, but I was terribly embarrassed. What the fuck was happening, as all my power gone away? And it would not come back and, in a way, to use a phrase, I was as helpless as a kitten.

Thomas had me to the vet, but there was nothing much that he could do. I think some steroids that picked me up, but only for a little while, and then I was falling down into the mess again.

We, by now, with Mammy at home, had gone through the winter; from September till May, when, and I know for me, Thomas gained a week's respite, with Mammy going back to hospital.

It should be mentioned that during this time it was not a one-man show. Far from it, for Mary was there for much of the time, if, because of her work, there was a limit to her involvement. Still, she did her best, what she could do in a hopeless situation, and afforded Thomas some off-time. But not enough to care for Mammy during his week's respite. Or what the doctor thought was a week's respite, for if Mammy was in a dreadful way, I was not much better. This fuck up, the whole thing, and if Thomas had thought that bringing Mammy could reverse time, to return thing back to how they used to be, he had to disappointed.

A strange thing, during all this time, her time at home, Mammy had ignored me. A complete indifference, as though I was not there. Why? I would think, right from the start, as one cripple to another one, that she knew my days were numbered and, as such, a new heartbreak for Thomas.

She went back in her wheelchair, into an ambulance, and later on that same day, I suddenly went blind. A total darkness. A human might have lost their mind, this affliction, but for me, in my dog's head, I accepted it with small alarm. The problem was I began to bump into things, walls and such, and Thomas asked, "What ails you, Martin?"

I can't see. And I could barely walk either, to go out, and I messed all over the place. In the house. As I had when I was small, a puppy. But I was coming then as I was going now, blind and lame and no way out, not this time, for Thomas.

"I don't want to lose you, Martin."

But I can't go on much longer.

"It will be the hardest thing I've ever done."

I know.

Our last night, and it was the first time I had seen Thomas cry. Great heaving sobs. We were sitting on the couch together – he had lifted me up, on to it – and I licked his face, his salty tears. *You are everything to me.*

We sat on the couch, a man and his dog; could you put it that way, all through the night together.

In the morning Thomas kissed the top of my head and carried me out to a waiting taxi. Our last time together, or close to it, and I was proud of Thomas, how he bore up. In the taxi and at the vets, where he stood at my side, holding me up to allow the vet to jag my front paw and seconds later I fell down dead. Or so they thought, and so did I. For a moment. For it was a terrible shock, the pain in my chest, before, in a clash of colour, and some colours never seen before, I was caught in a beam of light and whirling round the universe and back again and a vision of my body on the floor, on my side, in the vets. The vet was there but Thomas wasn't and I had to seek him out and I found him in a lane, drinking whisky.

All of this, as a whirl around the cosmos, the planets and stars and a glimpse through time, could you call it that, for time is non-existent. It had done for me when I was a dog, but I had now become an angel. A pure spirit. The trouble was that I could not relate to Thomas, who was the very picture of despair, drinking beer and whisky. What to do with my old pal, and I was new to the angel business. He could not see me if, I think, for I was very close, just above his head, he sensed my presence but shrugged it off for his imagination.

There was nothing I could do to tell him no, that it was not his imagination, that I was back and, in my new form, just above his head.

Steady up, Thomas.

But he continued to drink, in the morning in the lane and when he left the lane, he was not sober.

I followed him into an off sale, where he bought more booze and then went home.

I wish I could materialize.

In his chair in the house and all alone and I knew not how to comfort him, who, this harrowing day, or morning; for it was not yet ten in earthly time, sought escape in oblivion. So, there was nothing for it except to wait until he passed out, which, at the rate that he was drinking, would not take long. This new me and my new task as his guardian angel. As a whispered advice that I hoped he might heed if I knew it would not be easy. Anything but, and had he known the way I was, invisible, he would have had me robbing for him. And I would, if I could, have done it too. Why not? I was not a very holy angel. And it would have been fun, as Thomas and his *genie*. But that could not be and, in truth, I could see no way to help him. This is a problem for the dead that it is hard to help the living. When they refer to the deceased as departed, they are not kidding. We are out of the world, of existence, as they know it. But, and still; in whatever void, love endures forever. It was the reason I was back with Thomas, watching over him. In the very same house where, not long before, I had been an ailing dog. I was ailing no more but very sad, looking down on the hurting man who, I knew; by way of me, his putting me down, felt like a fucking murderer.

It was crazy, totally mad; but how to tell him that? The vet had tried, telling him that putting me down was an act of mercy. Which it was, and, for me, my only regret was leaving him. But it had to be, my decline and demise and Thomas should have known that. As Mammy did, I am almost sure, when sitting crippled in her chair. *Thomas's wee dog.* She had seen that I was old and almost toothless and, because she knew what I meant to him and the pain he would suffer when I was no more, it was too much for her to acknowledge me. Lucky for her that she was back in hospital and could not see the extent of it, his suffering. But I did. The heartbroken man. *I hate to see you this way, Thomas.* But he continued to drink to blunt his pain if he had to know that all the booze in the world could not bring me back again, not the way I used to be. His dog, Martin. The drinking, drunken, grieving Thomas who, so he thought, have left me lifeless on the floor in the veterinary surgery. Not so, and how I wished that I could tell him I was there, still with him, and, as sure as night will follow day, that we would meet again.

***

After a four-day drunk, he sobered up, as he had to do to take Mammy out of hospital. But, and another blow, Mammy suffered a further stroke on the morning of the very day she was due back home and could not leave the hospital.

By now, because of his drinking when he lost me, Thomas and Mary had fallen out and he was utterly, completely alone.

Mary was staying with friends, but he had no friends. There were some loose acquaintances, but no real friends and, should he die and join me there would be few people at his graveside. I would think just the priest and Mary. *Let no man write my epitaph.* No man would. Not for him. An unsociable cunt, to say the least. When I was a dog, I had copied him and it would have been a bold or stupid stranger who had thought to pat me. A snarling growl. *Leave me alone.* But it could well be that Thomas was learning when I was dead and Mary gone and Mammy stuck in hospital that it was better to have friends. Which he used to have when he was young. Had he died when he was ten or twenty or even while still under thirty there would have been a multitude in the chapel for his funeral. Morbid thoughts, but then he was far from cheerful.

***

Mammy was in a bad, bad way in hospital. It was called the Victoria Geriatric Unit in Mansionhouse Road in Glasgow. It is as well for humans that they can't see what they might come to. A good half of them would be in the Clyde – the river that runs through

Glasgow – or their head in a gas oven. Mammy had now lost her voice in the wake of her second stroke, but I think she knew that I was dead. Something about Thomas, that he was not the man he had been before, in the house while nursing her, or doing the best he could. I could see in her eyes her love for him and the frustration that she could not speak and ask him what was wrong. As for Thomas, he was not saying, telling her that I was gone and that he was sick in his very soul. A dog can do that to a man? In the surgery when I had collapsed by the barbiturate overdose Thomas had almost punched the vet, who had stood aside and a beseeching look that he did not hit him. A dangerous job, a vet, dealing with the likes of Thomas who, on the instant, but a blink too late, had changed his mind and now wanted to take me home with him. As it was, he contained his wrath, but it was touch and go that he had managed it. An angry man, angry at the vet, who, by then, was badly frightened but more sane than him. I was done and my time was up but Thomas could not accept it. My dear friend who rather than cry had threatened to explode. Still, he had got out of there with no damage done, for which I was more than grateful. Yes, and I was proud of Thomas that he had contained himself and had to wrecked the fucking place. For what it matters he would not, not ever, go anywhere near that place again because the memory was too painful.

So, well, to answer the question, a dog can do that to a man, and to even a tough one as Thomas was.

But Mammy sick in hospital he had to try to hide his grief if, as said, I would doubt that he was successful. Mammy, for all she was sick, knew him just too well. She was, was Mammy, it was all too clear, nearing the end of her earthly span. But Thomas still hoped for all she was ailing that she might come again. Another hope that would soon be dashed, for there was as little hope for her as there had been for me. At this time, and for the following months, Thomas was teetotal. Not a drop, because he was afraid to drink knowing what might happen. So, if a mighty effort, he abstained. His love for Mammy who, and unwell as she was, worried about him. Her wild son who, weighed down by sadness, had suddenly turned placid. That he could not fight against the fate of devastating happenings. This was a first for Thomas that, as time went on, he had finally given up and surrendered to what he could not change. The dead and dying, all that had once been his world. I could do nothing, only watch, as Thomas went his dreary way. Day after day, and sometimes twice a day, he would make his way to the hospital, a place of pain and suffering that he wished he had never seen.

It happened that a couple of months after my death one of the doctor's took a fancy to him. This woman, she was ages with him and quite attractive, went out of her way to speak to him and a fool would have known that – for whatever strange reason - she had more than a passing interest. Thomas more or less cold shouldered her, as, in all, myself and Mammy, had proved too much for him. This was a worry to me, his complete indifference to the doctor, for it was not like him at all. As something missing, gone out of him, since I had died. That and Mammy, if, by now, he had to know that there was very little hope for her.

She was fed up with it all, was Mammy. This hanging on. For what? Another dose of misery in the prison of her body, all twisted up and unable to speak and no way out because, and no matter what straits, there was no vet to rescue – what a word, but it is all too true – members of the human race.

For Thomas himself, at this time; full of gloom and more alone than he had ever been, death would have been a mercy. Not that I wanted him to die. Far from it. But I could feel his despair and, for companionship if nothing else, could only hope that she was successful in her try to interest him. This was the first since Mrs. Smart that a woman had had thrown herself at him. And a much better, fresher woman than that old hag had been. *Get in there, Thomas.* And he did, eventually, when I had all but given up on him. This new Thomas, for the old one would have been in there long ago. As it was, the doctor – what she saw in him, such a morose man, I'll never know; but then again you can never tell with women – waited for him outside the hospital and drove him home and asked *him* out.

***

Her name was Barbara and Thomas told her that Rocky Marciano had been married to a woman named Barbara.

"Who is Rocky Marciano?"

"He was the heavyweight champion back in the fifties."

Barbara said it was news to her. "I know nothing about

boxing."

Thomas said he did not know why he had mentioned it. "I didn't think that you'd be into boxing."

"But you are?"

"I must be. I've been to New York to watch it in the Garden."

"Do they box in a park?"

"No. Not in a park, a stadium. They call it Madison Square and it is in the centre of the city."

Barbara said she had never been in New York and Thomas said if she got the chance, she should visit it. "There's lots more to see than boxing."

"I would hope so." They were in a restaurant of Barbara's choice, where the staff knew her and, "They treat me well in this place."

Thomas said he seldom went out and was more into home cooking.

Home cooking, my arse; more beans and toast and fish and chips – you ought to be fucking honest

"You deserve to be treated well," he told Barbara. "I mean, you are a doctor and all of that."

"All of what?"

"Helping people, if you can."

"I sometimes can't?"

"You are helping me."

"I am?"

"You are."

"It's nice of you to say that."

"It's true."

"Tell me how, what way I am helping you?"

"Just being here, giving me your time."

"That's only because you are the saddest man, I think I've ever seen."

Thomas said that he had thought she was attracted to him. "But I shouldn't have, should I?"

"I think you know I'm attracted to you."

"I don't know why."

"Then that makes both of us because neither do I."

"Where do you think we go from here?"

"Your guess is as good as mine, where we go from here."

Thomas was stuck for words, so he said nothing.

Barbara said she had heard that he was a writer.

"I used to try to write."

"Used to?"

"I've written nothing for years."

"Is that because of writer's block?"

"I think it's more that I can't be bothered."

"I see."

"You do?"

"You are depressed."

"Right now, I am, but I wasn't depressed when I stopped writing."

"Did you feel you were not appreciated?"

Thomas laughed, and this more like he used to be and I was glad to see it. *Good on you, Barbara, for doing that if even unintended. He's had a rough, hard time since the loss of me and Mammy back in hospital and quarelling with Mary. I really hope they make it up for it is daft and they only have each other.*

Barbara asked had she said something funny?

"I never thought of it that way, appreciated."

"No?"

"Not in the slightest. I'm not what you could call a successful writer."

"I've heard of you."

"I don't know how."

"Someone in the hospital had a copy of one of your books."

"That's amazing. I've only published two books and they each sold less than fifty copies."

"It was a library book."

"I might have known. I think the Glasgow library's bought in six or seven copies."

"Still, you managed to write them, didn't you?"

"I suppose I did, but they're no great shakes."

That's not true, that you thought your books were no great shakes.

In the restaurant, eating – an awkward Thomas, because he was not used to dining out, to knives and forks and napkins – and he refused a glass of wine. "I'll make do with water."

Barbara said that was fine with her.

Thomas asked if she was married?

"No. I was, but I am now divorced. I live alone and have one daughter who is at university."

"I supposed she's studying medicine?"

"How did you guess, but, yes, she is. Her father is a doctor too, so it might run in the family." Barbara had Germanic look, blond hair and blue eyes and, for a woman of her age; I would think about fifty, she looked the goods; all trim and neat and a good catch for a man who had even half fancied a creature such as Mrs. Smart.

Thomas asked if she saw her daughter often?

"Not really. Her university is in Aberdeen, so she might come home only once a month. And when she does, she stays with her father."

This is getting better and better, Thomas.

Barbara smiling, sipping wine; and much more at ease than him. His glass of water and wanting a smoke, but thinking it better not to roll a smoke – I had never known him to buy a pack of cigarettes – in the restaurant. With Barbara. And what the fuck did she see in him? He was a man of the soil, the open spaces and not too good at small talk. Against that he had a certain manly, awkward charm that – as I well know – some women found appealing. They thought him honest, without guile? I would fancy more, as I had felt when I was with him, a feeling of protection. That they were safe when they were with him, if, in Barbara's case, she hardly needed his protection. But she had a good feeling none the less as was more than obvious, and, as she had said, she was attracted to him. My big pal who was a little bemused by all of this, for it had been a long, long time since any woman had showed an interest in him. What to do? He wanted Barbara as much or more than she wanted him, for he was fed up with his lonely bed, but – and this was before Viagra – let's just say that he was unsure, but ready for action just the same; for, as a lover will, he had washed and shaved and fresh new underwear. A rare occurrence these days, for he had lost all heart in everything and had not thought for romance and kisses. A new beginning? I hoped so, for I was not jealous of women now. They were a physical need for a man like him. Some-one to hold, to make love too.

Don't blow it, Thomas.

I, of course was listening in. My invisible perch atop his head. There was a first few grey hairs. It is the way of things, as monkeys in a cage, that the human race – who are no better than monkeys, and some of them a damn sight worse – just come and go too, when their time is up, surrender to a higher power.

Not that Thomas was near that yet. I would need to be patient for our eventual re-union. What a surprise to him, or maybe not. He might just say; "What, you again," before we sought out new adventures.

That in the future. But one sure thing it would come to pass, and, for me, the sooner the better for I was missing my old pal. The way we were, had been, and I had much to relate to him about my fantastic mission. My work as his guardian angel, which I would add all down the line had been far from easy. But stuck with him as, when I was a dog, he had been stuck with me. Our Tuesday nights at the novena. It was little wonder that I had felt familiar in the chapel and on the streets outside for I realised had been there before in, somewhat, the same guise that I am in now. And an easier time back then, when Thomas had been a boy. I had a couple of frights when, say, he had run out in front of traffic, but that is expected from a child. A knife in the back is another thing when that child becomes a man. There had been a few close things, and not only with knives, but hammers and, one time, a sword, and I must have been as good

197

at my job as Thomas had been when he was looking after me, a dog named Martin.

Thomas mentioned me to Barbara. "It almost killed me when he got old and I had to have him put to sleep."

Barbara said she had some idea of how much I must have meant to him. "But you can get another dog, you know."

Thomas said he supposed he could.

No, you can't; not one like me, you fucker!

"It might be the best thing you could do," Barbara said. Then. "I like dogs, too."

"You do?"

"I do."

"You would have liked Martin."

I don't think so.

Barbara asked about human friends. "Do you have any close ones?"

"No, not really."

"Why is that?"

"You tell me, you're the doctor."

"You're supposed to be a writer."

"I had lots of friends when I was young, and it might just be that I was disillusioned."

"That's interesting."

Do you really think so, Barbara?

"It might just be my nature, the way I am."

How true.

"Have you been married?"

"No."

"Why do you think that is?"

"I never found the right woman."

Barbara said she had never found the right man yet had still married. "It's what most people do."

"But I'm a fucking oddity."

"What?

"Sorry."

Barbara laughed. "I believe you are."

"I am."

"I think more unusual."

"That's a nicer way of putting it."

Barbara enquired if he had had woman problems.

"I suppose I have, but nothing desperate."

"Then you've been lucky."

"Good luck, bad luck, who knows?" Thomas said. "It is an old Jewish saying."

"A good one, too."

"I think it is."

Barbara said that Thomas had struck her as a devoted son. "You must love your mother very much."

"I do."

"How will you cope when she passes away?"

"I hope that she doesn't pass away for a long time yet."

"She's old, Thomas; and you have had her for a long time."

"Sometimes the longer you have some-one the more you want to keep them."

"You couldn't keep Martin, could you?"

"No, I couldn't keep Martin."

That's what you think.

"It could be something the same in regards to your mother."

"Are you trying to tell me something?"

"Nothing that you don't already know."

"I try not to think about it."

Barbara laid her hand on the back of his. "It's better to talk sometimes, you know"

Thomas said he knew it was but that he sometimes found it difficult. "It's like my whole world is crumbling away."

"You can talk to me, you know."

"I know.

He then asked her if she had read *Gone with the Wind* or seen the movie, and when Barbara said she had, both read the book and seen the movie, Thomas said that he felt something like Ashley Wilkes. "You know how Ashley yearned for the past, the old South, before the civil war."

Barbara said she would have never thought that. "Because you're not a bit like Ashley Wilkes."

"Maybe not, but I feel the same way he did, that my way of life is done for."

"It's a strange comparison."

"It only came to me just now."

"The same as Rocky Marciano, when you heard my name was Barbara?"

Thomas laughed. "That was crazy, wasn't it."

"But at least it's made you laugh."

"It's the first time I've laughed for ages."

"Then it was worth being crazy." Barbara signalled for the bill and, despite his protestations, insisted that the treat was on her.

"It was me who asked you out, after all."

"You're an astonishing woman, Barbara."

"That's a new one to me, astonishing."

"It shouldn't be."

"What does it mean?"

Thomas said surprising. "In a delightful way," he added.

"Have I helped your spirits?"

"You have."

Thank fuck for that, my dear friend; for I was beginning to despair for you, such a gloomy mood and for so long.

Barbara said she was glad to hear it, about his uplifted spirits. "You are a strange, deep man."

Thomas said she had caught him at a bad time. "I'm on a bit of a downer."

"I didn't expect you to be cheerful."

"Then you're not too disappointed?"

"I'm not disappointed in the least." Barbara looked him full in the eyes. "Do you want to come home with me?"

"I do."

Barbara's hand tightened on his. "No strings attached," she said.

A DOG'S OWN STORY

Get in there, Thomas.

***

I was pleased that the night went well. A sort of healing sex. It can sometimes happen and it happened for him that, for a time, he forgot his woes, his Mammy and me – my execution, for it was how he felt – and after sex he was at ease with Barbara who, too, for such a strange deep man, was at ease with him. Not, I don't think, that she still thought he was deep and strange. More that things had got on top of him and he had not known what way to turn and loneliness all around him. I felt sorry for my pal that, after all the years, he was a man alone. But a glimpse of hope with Barbara, that he might not be so alone any more.

I will not go into the nitty-gritty of their night together, except to say that it was good, no, better than good, and when, two nights later, they met again there were few formalities before they went to bed. This was more like the old Thomas, if, of course, he was still troubled. But a time of ease with Barbara, who, for her age – or for any age, come to that – was a luscious, full-bodied woman with no hang-ups. She enjoyed her sex, did Barbara. Even Thomas was surprised his, to him, delightfully lustful lover. But compassionate too and she would come to the chapel after Mammy died and her coffin was near the altar. *Ashes to ashes, dust to dust.* How true. From the womb to the tomb, or, in more recent times, it might be the crematorium. It hardly matters, mortal man, for either way they won't be coming back again.

***

Mammy passed away on a Saturday morning in May, 1993. Thomas had been at her bed in the hospital for almost all of the previous night, with Mary. Their relationship was still strained but at least they were speaking to each other now. This time of sorrow, of Mammy dying. There had been no mistake that she was dying, that her fight – and she had fought the stroke all down the line – was finally over. A little shrivelled-up old woman, comatose and full of morphine. It is a fact that hospitals give morphine to the dying.

Mary was with a couple of friends, while Thomas was alone. They had both been told to expect the worse, that Mammy might live for a couple of days and that they should both go home and get some rest. Mary and her friends left first while Thomas stayed until about three in the morning. This long night. Eventually, though, he phoned a taxi and went home. This was the lowest I had seen him since my own death at the vets. She always been there, had Mammy; all the time from the cradle up and this was to be a sore, sore loss; and nothing, not a thing he could do about it, to have Mammy live a little longer.

But, and something like me when I was at the vets; all my faculties gone, death would be a mercy to her.

Home at last – he had been in the hospital for twelve or fourteen hours – Thomas had only sat down when the telephone rang and he was told that Mammy had taken a turn for the worse and that he should return again to the hospital.

Could I speak, I would have told him that Mammy was already dead, but as it was I could only watch him. A telephone call for another taxi and post-haste to the hospital where he was told that she had died, and did he want to see her body? Thomas said no, and Barbara arrived – she must have told the hospital to phone her up in event of this, of Mammy dying – and they went home to her house where she did her best to comfort him.

"I couldn't bring myself to see her corpse."

"A lot of people feel the same."

"She's as well out of it, for her sake, but I will miss her terribly."

Barbara offered him some Valium. "It can help blunt the pain at a time like this."

Thomas shook his head at the offer of the Valium. "I knew it was coming and now I need to face it."

And so, he did. The arrangements for the funeral and the healing of his rift with Mary. It had been a silly, stupid falling out and I was happy to see that they were pals again and I am sure that Mammy – her spirit, that is – was happy too. Her children back together. In the chapel for her funeral mass. It was a quiet affair but dignified and very much in suiting for the woman she had been.

This, with Mammy in her coffin in the chapel is the end of my story, for to continue further would be more the story of a man, than the adventures of a man and dog.

Thomas Healy

Thomas Healy

5 Kerrycroy Avenue, Glasgow G42 0AA

Last night in Jerusalem

He had been fighting all his life, first bare-knuckle and then with gloves and at the age of twenty-two he beat a black American to become heavyweight champion. This, in many away, is the pinnacle in sports, and for a popular champion, the highest paid. Not, this sudden wealth and a worldwide fame, that he had changed too much and he played down his achievements. Eighty fights and eighty wins, almost all of them by knockout. This was a phenomenal record by any standards, and more especially now when he was thirty-eight years old. This is ancient for a boxer and Dan was more than aware of that. He had been hit and hit hard many times and he did not want to leave his wits in a boxing ring. No, and it had been his intention to have retired at thirty, but, some *lure*, he had gone on even if the fights were becoming harder. Not that any fight was ever easy. The beat of your heart before the bell. There is no mercy in the ring. You are all alone and if you fail, get beaten, then you'll be even more alone and lonely. For all his perfect record Dan was more than aware of that hard fact, and, this fear of defeat had made him an even tougher, harder man.

There had been talk of his retirement for the last five years, and his wife had said, "It's a young man's game, you can't go on forever." And that was true, but Dan thought another couple of years, and it was always that, another couple of years, five fights or six and then retire with dignity and pride." The greatest fighter who ever fought." He liked the praise, what had been written about him in countless publications and in many languages. He has come from nothing, from a council house in a housing scheme in Glasgow. Almost all great fighters had similar beginnings. Boxing is not a sport for the well-to-do. It never was and never will be. No sensible man wants a punch in the face. Dan had taken a few hard punches and the scars of old cuts patched his eyes and his nose was flatter than it should have been. For all of that he was a handsome man and definitely manly. Full of confidence. His manner and way and the way he walked, a rolling gait. Something like a cowboy would, or should. He was not exceptionally tall, around six feet; but the heft of him was something else, his neck and chest and wide, thick shoulders. The Heavyweight champion of the world, and he looked the part. In the ring and out of it.

Dan had been married for ten years and had two children, twin girls aged four. His wife had been a local girl and they had known each other all their lives and she could remember when Dan's mother had died when they were both nine years old. "My mammy is up there," he said, pointing to the sky. Brenda agreed with that and, even then, she was attracted to him and, when they were in their teens, they had begun to hang around together and, finally, when they both were in their thirties, had got around to marrying. In many a way it was an ideal match for she was well aware.